How to Make

L♥ve

Work

Michelle McKinney Hammond

How to Make
L♥ve
Work

**The Guide to Getting It,
Keeping It, and
Fixing What's Broken**

NEW YORK BOSTON NASHVILLE

Scripture quotations marked ASV taken from the *American Standard Version*.

Scripture quotations marked ESV are from the *Holy Bible, English Standard Version*, copyright © 2001 by Crossway Bibles, a division of Good News Publishers. Used by permission. All rights reserved.

Scripture quotations marked NASB taken from the *New American Standard Bible®*, Copyright © 1960, 1962, 1963, 1968, 1971, 1972, 1973, 1975, 1977, 1995 by The Lockman Foundation. Used by permission.

Scripture quotations marked MSG taken from *The Message*. Copyright © 1993, 1994, 1995, 1996, 2000, 2001, 2002. Used by permission of NavPress Publishing Group.

Scripture quotations marked NIV taken from the *Holy Bible, New International Version®*. Copyright © 1973, 1978, 1984 International Bible Society. Used by permission of Zondervan. All rights reserved.

Scripture quotations marked NKJV taken from the *New King James Version*. Copyright © 1982 by Thomas Nelson, Inc. Used by permission. All rights reserved.

Scripture quotations marked NLT are taken from the *Holy Bible, New Living Translation*, Copyright 1996. Used by permission of Tyndale House Publishers, Inc., Wheaton, Illinois 60189. All rights reserved.

FaithWords
Hachette Book Group USA
237 Park Avenue
New York, NY 10017

Visit our Web site at www.faithwords.com.

Printed in the United States of America

First Edition: June 2007
10 9 8 7 6 5 4 3 2 1

The FaithWords name and logo are trademarks of Hachette Book Group USA.

Library of Congress Cataloging-in-Publication Data
McKinney Hammond, Michelle, 1957–
    How to make love work : the guide to getting it, keeping it, and fixing what's broken / Michelle McKinney Hammond. — 1st ed.
        p. cm.
    ISBN-13: 978-0-446-58061-8
    ISBN-10: 0-446-58061-9
    1. Man-woman relationships. 2. Man-woman relationships—Religious aspects—Christianity. 3. Love. I. Title.
HQ801.M3425 2007
    248.4—dc22
                            2006039104

Here's to all those who are not afraid to pay the high price, unpack their hearts, and open themselves to loving as never before. May you be overwhelmed with delight at the awesome discovery of the fact that love is worth all the work after all.

Contents

Contents

Troubleshooting   231

Acknowledgments

To my new publishing family at FaithWords. Thank you for giving me the awesome opportunity to expound on my favorite subject. Anne Goldsmith, Holly Halverson, and Heidi Nobles, thanks for coming to the rescue—we did it! Hey, Rolf, keep running. There's triumph in there between the agony and the victory you feel when you've completed something that tests everything within you. Thanks for believing in this book! Beth Jusino, you are awesome and wonderful in every way: you are the master agent. Thanks to my family for putting up with me when I turn into the writing hermit. My inner circle, my prayer mavens, my staff, and all my Diva girls—you know who you are, so hopefully you know how much you mean to me, 'cause trust me, I couldn't do what I do without you. You have my heart as well as my deep and speechless appreciation.

Lord, You are so much more than Lord to me. I love You. I enjoy You, and I stand in awe of You and all that You are able to do through me. I feel so undone, but I am determined to keep showing up and hopefully doing something that puts a smile on Your face as often as I can. I so totally belong to You and it's good to know You feel the same way. You are the love of all loves, and it feels good to be known and loved by You. I remain addicted to Your Presence.

Who can say
            When one will find love
A minute
            An hour
                        A lifetime from now
            Just beyond your faith
                        Your impatience
                        Your surrender to His divine clock
                        Tick, tick, ticking
                                    On the mantle of your heart
Who can say
            How you will find it
                        Love
By sliding into it
            The way a ballplayer
                        Who's covered all the bases
                        Glides across the plate
                                    Claiming victory for the home team
            Or inching into it
Testing the temperature with your toes
                        Until you are convinced
                        That the water is fine
Fine as wine
            That you taste
                        Rolling it on your tongue
                                    While you swirl it around in the glass
                                    Letting it breathe
                                    Just enough
                                                To give you pleasure
                                                When you take
                                                            Another sip
                        And another
            And another
                        Until you are intoxicated by the flavor
            Or the aroma
                        Who can tell
            They merge together
                        Warming you
                                    Filling you

With irrepressible delight
That would be love
But how to find it
How to find it
How *do* you find it?
Love
Do you hunt for it?
Track it?
Stalk it?
Kidnap it?
And hold it for ransom
Until it complies with your wishes
Or do you coax it out of hiding
Luring it
With tantalizing treats
Decadent secret delights
And tasty promises of
To have and to hold
Forever and ever
Amen
Or do you
Reach out tentatively
Eyes squeezed shut
Not daring to look
Because you're not quite sure of where . . .
Where to find love
Now that is the question
Under a soft pillow
Perhaps in the same place
The tooth fairy used to leave a reward
In exchange for a small piece of you
A piece of you
That you were reluctant to lose
Until you discovered
It was not so bad after all
As you made room
For something new to grow in its place
Where to find love
Good question

Everywhere
Nowhere
Somewhere warm and safe
Perhaps tucked beneath the arm of God
Close to His heart for safekeeping
Like a diamond is kept
Guarded from thieves
Those who are undiscerning of its value
And those who are not
Willing to pay the price
It is kept
For the right day
The right time
The right setting
Because it's all about who
Who you will love
And who you will become
In order to be loved
You see
In order to receive love
You must *give* love
In order to give love
You must *have* love
In order to find love
You must *know* love
Know God
Know love
Intimately
Passionately
In order to recognize it
Recognize Him
Recognize love
Which raises the question
What does love look like anyway?
Is it as breathtaking
As the rising and setting of the sun?
As beautiful as a flower
That draws us closer
To inhale its fragrance?

As cleansing as the rain?
Or does it simply look like you
Like me
Like God?
Constantly changing to fit the appropriate vessel
So it matters not what, where, when, or how
It only matters who
Who you know
And that is where we make the incredible discovery
That love has been
Available
Watching
Waiting
Within reach
All along
No great mystery after all . . .

Introduction: The Big Picture

There I sat in the middle of the floor, wondering why the cabinet I had just put together didn't look like the one on the box. It was the same color, yes. It had a similar shape. But something was wrong with it. The one on the box stood straight and looked solid. It promised to hold a lot of things I was looking forward to putting inside of it. But my cabinet looked a little sad as it leaned to one side, resembling the Tower of Pisa. As I opened one of the doors, it came off in my hand. I wondered if one of the extra screws that sat next to me belonged in the extra hole I now studied.

What had I done differently from the manufacturer?

Just as I was about to conclude that I had been given a defective piece of merchandise, my assistant asked, "Did you read the instructions?"

"No," I replied. "I know what it's supposed to look like!"

"Well," she said, studying my face, "knowing what it's supposed to look like and knowing how to put it together are two different things."

I pursed my lips and thought about what she said. It had seemed simple enough when I first opened the package. All the basic pieces were there. I laid them out in the order I thought was best for putting them together and went to work.

It was true that I hadn't been able to figure out where a few pieces went, but they seemed inconsequential. Now, the evidence that my lack of knowledge had indeed affected the outcome of my project was glaringly evident. Slowly I took the cabinet apart and spread the pieces out before me. Then I unfolded the instructions and studied the diagram.

"Oh, that's what this piece is for!" I exclaimed. I noticed my assistant was struggling to keep a straight face. My pride stung a little as I rearranged the pieces according to the instructions. I finally completed my project, and I had to admit it looked and worked a lot better than the previous construction.

So what was the lesson I learned from all of this? Just because you think you know what it's supposed to look like doesn't necessarily mean you know how to get the end result you desire. I find it interesting that we study to do everything else on the face of the earth except the most important one—building healthy, fulfilling relationships. Who really tells us how to put two people together? Or better yet, how to *keep* them together?

Many of today's movies show us how to manipulate people's emotions to the point that they finally raise their hands in defeat and run for cover *or* fall madly in love *or* at least move out of their parents' houses. But are any of these tactics realistic, or are they just cute ideas for the movies?

I certainly don't want to be manipulated, and I can't think of anyone else who does, either. Love is a very delicate matter. Our hearts are strong yet fragile. Pain in this most complex part can be worse than pain anywhere, and we take longer to recover from it.

When it comes to capturing and keeping the love we've always wanted, there is no easy 1-2-3 formula. But there are certain principles that work. I'm not talking about the stuff movies are made of but about sound principles, established by the One who created us and knows how we are wired. Yes, the Master Manufacturer, God, has a lot to say about love—what works and what doesn't.

But before we go any further, you have a decision to make. Are you willing to throw away all of your assumptions about matters of the heart, all of your preprogramming according to popular culture? Everything your friends have said? Everything you've observed?

Are you ready for a brand-new, radically different set of directions that will show you what it takes to put two people together and keep them together? Most important: are you willing to *follow* the instructions?

If you're wavering on this point, answer these questions: How far has trying to figure it out on your own gotten you? Has the advice of others gotten you what you wanted so far? Are you happy yet?

If it's true that doing the same thing over and over again while expecting different results is insanity, then it is definitely time to try something new. So stop the madness and get wise. Let's stop guessing and get a set of instructions that works.

I suggest that we go back to the Bible, the official Manufacturer's Instruction Manual for life, to find principles that have worked for as long as men and women have been roaming the face of the earth. Whether you believe that the Bible is the Word of God, whether you have an intimate relationship with God, the bottom line is that the principles found in His Book are universal truths. They work whether you believe in them—or Him—or not.

Therefore, no matter what you believe, you should remain open to the principles the Bible offers for human relationships. If you want love—real, lasting, fulfilling love—you've got to read the Manual!

The fact is that though love is a very emotional thing, you must use your head along with your heart to attain the love you not only want but need. So proceed with caution. Nothing about these instructions is hazardous to your health, but they might revolutionize your thinking, which I'm sure you won't mind as long as they work!

What This Guide Will Do

We have chosen to consult with the Manufacturer about this thing called love and find out what is in His Manual (that would be the Bible) to create this owner's guide. This guide is practical, with easy-to-read instructions that are sure to help you make love work.

Still, you may be surprised by some of the instructions God gives. Before you toss them aside, though, consider who wrote them. Remember that He knows the most about love and relationships because He created them in the first place.

This guide will reveal some of the hidden features of relationships. It will also lead you through some of the more elusive and mysterious ins and outs of love and how it works—that is, if you want it to last.

This guide will also help you recognize the various parts required to make love work and give you the instructions for assembly and maintenance.

For those of you with more complex issues, I have provided a Troubleshooting section. It will help you figure out what's wrong and, more important, it will help you fix the problem.

As with any instruction manual, when all else fails, you always have tech support. Should you choose to use the Help Hotline, you will find the Master Operator eternally available, a sure help in times of need.

Last, but certainly not least, keep in mind that these instructions will not work through osmosis. In order for anything to function properly, you must follow the directions deliberately and consistently. Sometimes it takes a while for all the pieces to line up and run smoothly, but don't allow this to deter you from doing your part. As you work toward getting love up and running in your life, you will be amazed at the changes that take place, first in you and then in those around you. Get ready to become a love magnet!

1

Parts

"The body is a unit, though it is made up of
many parts; and though all its parts are many,
they form one body."
—1 CORINTHIANS 12:12 NIV

- You
- The Man
- God
- The Heart
- The Soul
- The Mind
- Strength

You

Y ou are incredible, and You were made for love! David wrote, "I praise you because I am fearfully and wonderfully made; your works are wonderful, I know that full well" (Ps. 139:14 NIV).

As we consider all the pieces required to make love work, the part You will notice first is You. Not Sally, Mary, or John—just You. You may seem to be the most important piece, but You must note that each piece has equal power in the love equation. You have to give as much power as You want to receive. If one piece is missing or not operating at full capacity, love will either malfunction or fail to work at all.

Know How to Use the Part

To use the pieces correctly, You must identify and study each of them. In the case of the part called You, you'll need to do three things: know yourself, like yourself, and be yourself.

Know Yourself

Umm-hm, I know that sounds simple, but it really isn't. It is amazing how many people really don't know themselves. Several years ago, I logged on to a dating Web site out of curiosity. As I completed the personality profile, I was stunned. There were dimensions of myself I had never considered! Things that were important to me. Things I hated. Things I liked. But most of all, who I was. The deeper into the profile I got, the clearer it became why my past relationships had not worked. I had chosen to go with the flow in each relationship without ever being clear about the things that were deal-breakers or deal-makers for me. The test forced me to consider and define what I had to have and what I couldn't stand in my partner and relationships. Knowing this up front can help You avoid experiencing unnecessary pain and wasting precious time on a no-win situation.

Knowing who You are is huge because if You don't know yourself, it will be hard for anyone else to get to know You. After all, how can You share your heart if You don't know what's really in it?

Don't do another thing or attempt to begin another relationship until You get to know yourself, including the good, the bad, and the ugly. Make a list of what You must have to celebrate yourself, your life, and another person. The nonnegotiables, the things you're willing to work with, what You can't stand, and what You can live without.

If these things don't come to mind immediately, consider completing a personality profile or a temperament test, or simply journal your rambling thoughts on love and life. Just do whatever You have to do to know yourself. This one big step will definitely clarify what You need to look for when it comes to love and help You locate it more readily.

Like Yourself

Another biggie. I have to confess that for a long time I did not like myself. Then why on earth did I expect anyone else to like me? I constantly pointed out my own flaws when entering new relationships, thinking I would garner compassion. Instead, I got disdain. My suitors tended to agree with my list of flaws, even if they hadn't noticed these problems until I mentioned them! Take it from the voice of experience: if someone doesn't notice your flaws, don't You dare tell!

Humans don't handle flaws very well, but the Manufacturer does. Man looks at the outward appearance, but thank God that He looks at our hearts! After all, since He made You, He knows everything about You and is not rocked by defects. We all have them. Yes, sorry to break it to You—you're only human. This should be a relief to You! So clap your hands, dance, sing, and celebrate your official release from the pressure to be perfect because the truth is that You cannot be. You are not wired for perfection, but You *are* wired to love and to be loved in spite of your flaws.

Sure signs that You do not like yourself include low self-esteem, insecurity, a critical spirit, and the inability to accept love when it is extended to You. You will have to be honest with yourself to acknowledge that You struggle with any of these issues, but when You do, You will have taken your first step toward freeing yourself for love.

In order to overcome this debilitating state of mind, You must do what the Manufacturer recommends. He does not suggest but *orders* You to love yourself. Self-loathing is not an option built into your internal hard drive. He knows You can't love others until You love yourself. It is actually an insult to His creation when You don't love yourself because when He created You, He called You a good thing! In His mind, everything He creates is good. Therefore, You need to say over and over what He says about You until it becomes part of your internal programming.

Repeat after me: "[Oh God, You made me as I am on purpose!] 'You formed my inward parts; You knitted me together in my mother's womb. I praise You, for I am fearfully and wonderfully made. Wonderful are your works'" (Ps. 139:13–14 esv). Now hug yourself and make friends with guess who? You.

Be Yourself

Remember that You want another person to fall in love with You. The real You. Chameleons are lizards, not people. Trying to be anyone other than yourself is false advertising. Plus, it's hard work keeping up all that pretense. At some point, the real You will emerge, and You will have one hot mess if the other person decides that You are not what he bargained for. In the function of love, counterfeit parts will not work. They will only tangle the cord that supplies the power to love. So take a good, hard look at yourself. Are You true to yourself and your spirit when you're around others? Especially when you're trying to impress a potential love interest? Do You go against your own grain and make yourself uncomfortable by following the crowd to fit in? Are You comfortable in the skin you're in? Are You an authentic original or a cheap copy of someone else?

If You need help with being yourself, please go to the Manufacturer's Instruction Manual (the Bible) to see that He designed You to be an extraordinary expression of His love. The Manufacturer has made each person unique on purpose. Humans are a tribute to His masterful creativity.

The thing is, if You know yourself, like yourself, and understand why You were created, You won't find it hard to be who You really are.

How Do You Fit into the Mechanism of Love?

Let's examine this part called You thoroughly. What do You look like and how do You fit into the assembly of this thing called love?

You are crucial to the design of love. You see, You were created by love for the amazing, fabulous purpose of loving, which is why You crave love so much. You can't help yourself. Regardless of how many bad experiences You've had in the romance department, and though your mind may war against the concept, your heart still overrules and screams, "Admit it: You want to be loved, You need to be loved, You can't live without love!"

And that, my friend, is the truth. You cannot get away from the core of who You are—a lover. It is imprinted on your DNA. The Master Manufacturer crafted every fiber of your being to give and receive love. These actions are the greatest evidence that You know your Creator, "for love comes from God. Everyone who loves has been born of God and knows God" (1 John 4:7 NIV). For this reason, no matter how gifted we are, He has no reason to be impressed unless we love well (see 1 Cor. 13:1–3).

Love is the one program You cannot erase from your personal hard drive. It is part of the original programming. For millennia, men and women have lived, fought, and died for this invisible yet over-whelmingly powerful thing called love. How many songs have been sung, movies made, and poems and books written chronicling every aspect of love? 'Nuff said.

Obviously, this obsession is not momentary. It is who You are. Love will be your ultimate quest in life and your crowning accomplishment. No matter how much money You make or what You achieve, the bottom line will be how much You love others and others love You.

> We become the sum total of the love we are able to give and inspire in our lifetimes.

Small wonder this one area of our lives seems the most problematic.

Please note that while it is perfectly normal for You to have the desire to love, You should never allow the desire for love to have You. If desire rules You, You will malfunction—make bad choices that ignore the Manufacturer's Manual—and short-circuit the pos-sibility of receiving the very thing You so deeply desire.

Ah, 'tis true: "Desire without knowledge is not good, and whoever makes haste with his feet misses his way. When a man's folly brings his way to ruin, his heart rages against the LORD" (Prov. 19:2–3 ESV). Newsflash: these verses are true for women, too. It's not God's fault. You've got to own your stuff—including your choices—if You want to make changes in your life!

So what about You? You, whom God fashioned and made for love? There are a few things that You must understand about your-self before beginning your quest for love.

You Have the Power to Invite or Repel Love

For the most part, You attract what You are. This truth can be pain-ful to absorb, but it is still truth. People instinctively know what they can get away with in your presence. They follow your cues. If You don't demand commitment and respect, for example, then they won't give it. Get the picture? Make it clear what You want, need, and expect from the relationship, and don't settle for anything less.

Two caveats: (1) Never demand what You are not willing to give yourself; and (2) Remember that the man's potential should not influence your initial evaluation of him. How he begins is a good indication of how he will finish. In other words, what You see is what you'll get. Consider him an "as is" purchase.

You should also allow a limited time to chart diminishing returns when he's no longer on his best behavior to impress You. That's when you'll see the real person You may eventually live with.

So where does that leave You as You look over the terrain of your past relationships? What patterns do You see? What is the state of your heart? Where You are right now is where your own choices have led You. One of the most precious gifts the Manufacturer has given You is free choice.

If You are beginning to backpedal, violently shake your head, and say, "No, this is not true. I did not choose to be where I am right now," I urge You to consider this. Whether You say yes or no, You make a choice. Whether You say anything at all or not, you've made a choice. If You do nothing, You make the choice to do nothing. You can actively participate in the pursuit of love, or You can passively sit on the sidelines and watch the parade pass You by. Either way, it's a choice.

When people ask me why I'm not married yet, I tell them it's a choice. I could be married if I wanted to be, but thank goodness I get to choose when, where, and whom I marry! So do You.

The Needs of You

You Need to Admit You Need Love

In order to make the right choices, You must be honest with yourself about the fact that You need love. Again, needing love is not something You get to quibble about with the Manufacturer. You can relax. You have permission to desire and need love. This need is an essential part of your being, the essence of yourself.

Yes, You need to feel a profound connection to someone other than yourself. It was the Manufacturer who first uttered those profound words: "It is not good for the man to be alone" (Gen. 2:18 NIV). That verse also covers women. Woman was made as a helpmate for man. This fact should be empowering. You read it in Genesis, folks, so it's official: even God Himself knows that men need help! And guess what? You need help, too.

If You are selfish, this revelation could be a shock to your system. Still, it is something You are destined to discover because selfishness always leads to loneliness. Needing love is what Genesis 2:24—"and the two are united into one" (NLT)—is all about. It is about connecting, living, and breathing inside of someone else. Hearing his heartbeat and his dreams. Being part of his internal life, where You exchange secrets and plans. It is the electric sensation of possessing someone and being possessed by him in a way that brings meaning to your life.

When two people can say to each other, "I am connected to you. I am better because you are in my life," light shines in their eyes. This connection can be present in a romance or in a relationship with God or a friend. The human desire for companionship is huge and becomes the driving force behind significant decisions and even mundane ones. This longing for connection is central to your makeup, your wiring.

Though You are designed to be a complete piece on your own, You can, when connected to the right piece, experience additional power operating in your life. King Solomon said it best when he noted that two were better than one because they had a good return for their labor (see Eccl. 4:9). Connecting to the wrong piece can short-circuit a fuse, damage your internal hard drive, and cause You to shut down for an undetermined amount of time—or even crash permanently.

You Need a Security System

This part called You needs a security system for protection. Everyone needs someone to rely on. A revolving door of relationships is unhealthy because it breeds insecurity, fear of abandonment, commitment problems, and a host of other maladies that affect every other area of life. Though You may crave variety and the stimulation it brings, You must feel safe.

Your inner circle—your security system—does that. Those people become the period at the end of your sentence and make the declaration of who You are a final statement. They reinforce and "name" You the way that Adam named Eve (see Gen. 2:23). The name he gave her added to the meaning of who she was and didn't take away from her original design.

If we look at the example of Jesus' relationships, we see that though He reached out to the world at large, He also focused on individuals He met along the way. In addition, He had a closer circle of faithful followers (the disciples) and a select group who were even closer (Peter, James, and John). Finally, there was only one who knew everything about Him—His heavenly Father, God. It was with God that Jesus was completely vulnerable.

This is the model for your relationships. You will have your acquaintances, your friends, your family, and the one with whom You share all. Notice that the one You choose to share your secrets with—the nurturer and guardian of the inner You—has the greatest effect on who You are. "As iron sharpens iron," family, friends or life partners will shape and mold one another (Prov. 27:17 NIV). They will help remove the rough edges if we open ourselves up to being transformed by love and partnership.

The person You choose to love and spend the rest of your life with will (hopefully) change You, name You, define You, and add a dimension to your world that did not exist previously. Contact with and submission to this person should transform You into a You that is greater than before. At least that is the Manufacturer's intention! Love will always take You to a higher place than where You presently dwell. It should elevate your mind and, ultimately, your quality of living.

Establish your security system—those on whom You can rely to help You stay sane and safe in the pursuit of love. Look for those who help You, as a part, run efficiently.

You Need Significance

Every woman on the face of the earth longs to feel that she's made her mark. She needs to feel that she matters not just to the universe or to her circle of peers. She must also know that she truly, truly matters to someone special, someone she can call her own. Go on, tell the truth: You need to feel desired by someone! You need to feel as if You add the oxygen to someone's breath.

We all can live without a lot of things, but air is not one of them. God breathed into man and made him a living soul (see Gen. 2:7). Without God's breath, he would have been only a mound of clay, beautifully fashioned but still just lying there.

The Manufacturer has made You not only to love but also to be an agent of change. The first thing God did after creating Adam and Eve was to give them their marching orders: "Be fruitful and multiply and fill the earth and subdue it and have dominion over the fish of the sea and over the birds of the heavens and over every living thing that moves on the earth" (Gen. 1:28 ESV).

In other words, maximize your creative ability, take care of what I've created, exercise the authority I've given You, master self-control, and establish order; now go forth and handle it! We pursue our purposes so passionately because God instructed us to. *What on earth am I here for?* is the burning question for all time. Significance is huge and defining. Yet significance is not enough.

Many a sister who has prided herself on arriving professionally and financially has made the stunning discovery that she swallowed a big fat lie—the lie that focusing on professional success first and foremost is the answer. Having accomplished her professional goals, she is faced with a profound truth: success doesn't satisfy if You don't have anyone to share it with. Whew! Tell the truth and shame the devil—You want and need love, to be a significant part of someone else's world! Again, the need for significance and love is part of your built-in programming that cannot be erased or reset.

You Need to Grow

Next, You need to grow, to evolve as a person spiritually, emotionally, and intellectually. You cannot grow on your own. Other people are the agents of growth. God may build You as a part, but others will whittle and hone You to a lean, mean, smooth-running machine. Through conflict and maddening habits, others will level your rough parts and make You function well with other parts.

Oh yes, my friend, it is the function of all relationships to make You grow. You may not always like what your loved ones say to You, but if they speak the truth in love, their words should help You to grow up in all things, which is exactly what the Manufacturer intended (see Eph. 4:15).

Caution: some will distort You and warp your program (your sensibilities) rather than helping You grow—if You let them. Spend enough time with someone who doesn't operate well herself, and You will find your rough spots getting rougher. Some people stifle your growth by refusing to grow themselves. These are just pieces of waste getting into your mechanism, and You need to throw them out. Remember 1 Corinthians 15:33: "'Do not be deceived: bad company ruins good morals'" (esv).

Those who have embraced their drive to grow will make the painful decision to leave bad influences behind. Again, don't feel guilty. You will be held responsible for the company You keep because it has such a strong effect on You—and because your gift of choice is involved, You will never be able to blame your lack of growth on another person.

Remember that if You are not growing—getting strong and operating smoothly with use and working well with other parts—You are corroding. And decay will always lead to death. "This relationship is killing me" is not a good thing to utter unless it means You are losing the selfish portions of yourself. If a relationship is causing the good parts of You to jam, wear down, or rust, it may be time for some troubleshooting. (See the Troubleshooting section for more instruction.)

You *Need to Contribute*

Finally, You need to make a contribution to someone. We are blessed in order to be a blessing. To horde all of your goodness for yourself is a sin. Giving really is better than receiving (see Acts 20:35). You were made to share yourself and all that is within You with someone else so another part can function more productively and happily. Therefore, You must examine carefully why You want a relationship.

If a relationship is just about what You will *get*, I suggest You not move forward with assembly. The device is sure to break down because one end (the other person in the relationship with You) will bear all the weight and receive no help from the other end (You).

Love is not for takers. In order for love to work, both people in the relationship must contribute 100 percent to its operation. The part continually receiving the short end of the stick will short-circuit from being overtaxed. The wear and tear will cause your partner to break down. And one working part plus one broken part equals no function at all. Love is halted.

Look at it this way: You as a part have prongs that face outward. Therefore, You should be looking for somewhere to plug in, somewhere to give and supply power.

Some Facets of You

Now that we've identified what your needs are, let's talk about how You work best.

You *Must Function Independently of Other Parts*

You cannot be connected to any attachment that hinders your capacity to love as You should. You must be freestanding and passionately

engaged with the main Power Source of love—the One who made love Himself, the Master Manufacturer, God.

You Can Connect to Only One Partner

While connected to the Power Source, You can be joined to just one other romantic part at a time. To experience the best results, keep yourself free from past relationships, present distractions, extraneous and irrelevant matter, baggage, and unresolved issues that could harm your relationship.

You Get the Ball Rolling

You must dare to get out of the box, remove the wrapper, and be open to the endless possibilities for love that await You. Rest assured that the Manufacturer knows the plans He has for You! They're fabulous "plans for wholeness and not for evil, to give You a future and a hope" (Jeremiah 29:11 ESV). Prepare to live, love, and learn.

Okay, we've examined You the part: the need to be authentic and not a knockoff, to love and be loved, to have a security system for protection, to grow in order to avoid stagnation (decay), to contribute to other parts in the mechanism of love. Next, let's look at what the other half of this love apparatus should look like, how it should function, and what it should add to You. A lot will depend on aligning with the right part in the right way at the right time—if You really want love to work.

INSIDER'S LOVE TIP
You must be "right" to be able to see and receive one who is right for You. The person You align yourself with has everything to do with who You are.

The Man

T he MAN part can cause YOU the most angst, wonder, and joy all at the same time. This piece is the one you're looking for. This piece can fulfill YOU, destroy YOU, or make YOU blow a fuse. In order to connect to this piece properly, YOU must first identify it. YOU might not recognize it if YOU are looking for a piece with outward-facing prongs (which YOU may be because we all start out looking to receive love). This piece actually has slots for insertion instead. YOU need to get real when it comes to this piece. Every single woman is looking for the same thing YOU are: someone to fill in the empty spaces in her world, to balance her and bring a sense of completion. So understand and know that YOU are not alone in your search for this part.

What YOU Bring to the MAN—and Vice Versa

The MAN Needs YOU

The MAN needs what YOU bring to the mechanism called love. YOU will give him strength. If you are joined together at the right time, YOU will enable him to operate at his full potential. If you are connected too early—if either YOU or he is not prepared—damage may occur to both parts. As I always say, the right person at the wrong time can feel like the wrong person at any time. Truly, timing is everything.

You *Need the* Man

This person adds to You, fills in the blanks in your life. If the Manu-facturer has selected him for You, You and the Man will be empow-ered to fulfill God's purposes for your lives as a couple. This pairing is not exclusively a mate thing. People who are not romantic parts will also contribute to your destiny.

> Though You were created to be whole without the Man, the Manufacturer has wired You to be desirous of and even dependent on additional sources of power, lest You get a big head and begin to believe that You are all that and a bag of chips all by yourself.

Trust me—You could always use a little more seasoning.

The Manufacturer designed each person to function differently, so when two partners are joined together, they become a danger-ous team, actually increasing each other's power. "And the two are united into one" (Gen. 2:24 NLT) takes on a whole new meaning when You see that two people joining together could cause a power explosion!

The power You and the Man share depends on the amount of power each of You can generate in any given moment. What does that mean? Some days, You are going to be filled with love beyond measure for the other person. Some days, You won't, and the Man won't, either. This situation could either make the relationship re-ally interesting or put it in danger.

There will be fluctuations in the current of your relationship from time to time, depending on what other sources are attempting to draw power from You or the Man. Things such as jobs, family pres-sures, and financial issues can overload either person's fuses, causing a shutdown or a blowup.

And You will notice, as You become closer, that this MAN not only has slots for receiving but also has outward prongs to give power, as love is an endless series of give and take.

What Matters, and What Doesn't

Keep in mind that the MAN needs and wants all the same things You do. Those are, in short review, the needs to connect, experience consistency and stimulation, feel a sense of significance, to experience growth, and contribute something to someone other than himself. If the MAN experiences all these things while he is with You, he will fall head over circuits in love with You and fuse himself to You forever.

In order for the connection between You and the MAN to work, the MAN needs to be like You, yet different; he must be the same in his inner core but different in function. Temperaments and occupations can be different, but your values need to be as similar as possible. This truth is important. Opposites attract, but in most cases, they cannot maintain a long-term connection because they are not really compatible. They burn each other out because of the extreme amount of power needed to compensate for all their differences. It simply takes way too much energy to try to get along with someone You don't agree with! Let's face it: agreement is important.

I'm not talking about agreeing on politics; that's external stuff. Think about the stuff that will hit closer to home: how You spend your money, how You will raise your children, how You keep your home, the things You truly value—shall I go on? Those who operate on the same wavelength maintain a consistent balance that increases productivity, joy, peace, overall satisfaction with life, and longevity in the relationship. This is Scripture sprung to life: "Can two walk together, unless they are agreed?" (Amos 3:3 NKJV).

What the other person looks like is not important. It really isn't! As You should know by now, good things, as well as a lot of power, can come wrapped in the most unexpected packages. I once liked just a certain physical type of MAN. I dated this type over and over in various sizes, shapes, and colors, only to find myself back where I had begun, looking for yet another person.

And then one day it happened. One MAN who was *not* my type externally snuck in and swept me off my feet. He was the opposite of everything I had ever been attracted to before. I can honestly say I wouldn't have looked at him twice walking down the street, but he had me wrapped around his finger with a little bow. And that is when I learned an important lesson—the cover of a book is no indication of the amazing contents.

Warning: revisiting the type that doesn't work can be very unhealthy. Many have mistakenly chosen what they thought was their missing piece over and over again only to find that love did not work. Those women become disillusioned and give up on every prospect of love. This is totally unnecessary, for love can never be wasted, even if it is not reciprocated according to your liking. YOU should never get tired of doing good, because you'll eventually reap what YOU sow—so make sure you're sowing a lot of love (see Gal. 6:9).

Keep looking with an open heart. Never let another person make YOU give up on love. Love is infinitely more powerful than any person YOU will ever meet because it is an inherent part of the GOD piece. This piece will always be in place, whether or not YOU are connected to any other parts (or partners). This piece was, is, and will remain in place, connected securely to YOU, no matter who does or does not love YOU, for as long as YOU choose to accommodate it.

By the time YOU complete the Parts section, I hope you'll feel empowered to be more discerning about whom YOU choose to align yourself with and what will work for YOU in your love connection.

In conclusion, I hope YOU now understand that to enjoy optimum power in making love work, YOU need to look for a MAN who is like YOU (at heart) but different from YOU (in gifts and function). YOU know now not to write someone off because of his appearance. (I wouldn't blame YOU if YOU hoped for someone who is handsome, but love has the capacity to transform your potential partner into someone beautiful in your eyes. Love has been known to cover a multitude of flaws and sins (see 1 Pet. 4:8). And now you're ready to look at another vital part of this exquisite device called love: its Ultimate Power Source!

INSIDER'S LOVE TIP
The MAN has the same needs You do. But he is equipped to give only what he has received from his former connections. Therefore, it would be wise to wait until You have more information on his former configurations before attempting to download him into your heart.

GOD

N ow we're talking about the central Source of power. Many have tried and failed to make love work without this very special component. A lack of power reminds me of the story about the woman who bought a high-end refrigerator. After getting it home, she was furious to find it wasn't working. The representative she spoke with at customer service instructed her to check several things, all to no avail. Finally, the rep asked her to see if the refrigerator was plugged in. The woman returned to the phone embarrassed but indignant, stating that for the amount of money she had paid for the refrigerator, it should have worked whether she had plugged it in or not!

Many tend to feel the same way about love. It should work whether or not they are plugged in to the One empowering them to keep the love connection alive and strong.

There are a few things You need to know about the GOD part.

The GOD Part

GOD Is Always the Same
This piece has always been. It is the only piece that is not manufactured or created and has no need for upgrades. It is superior to all the other parts, programs, and applications. This is your Power Source, so without it, the rest of your system cannot function. The GOD piece invigorates all the other parts and never breaks down. It is solid through and through and has been known to keep on loving even when the

parts connected to it break down. This is the only part that cannot be exchanged or replaced. Psalm 100:5 reminds us that "His steadfast love endures forever, and his faithfulness to all generations" (ESV).

God Is Love

"For God so loved the world . . ." (John 3:16 NIV). God loves love and wants everyone to experience the power and the joy of it. Therefore we need Him in order to function correctly when attempting to put two hearts together. Remember: everything operates as an extension of this main Power Source. If we are disconnected from this power, our ability to make love work—last and fulfill us and our partners—is diminished greatly. We can operate on our own power for only so long before our batteries run out. (We will visit solutions for this malfunction in our Troubleshooting section.)

Before You Love the MAN, You Must Love GOD

God created us all to give and receive love. But there is an order to the assembly. You and the MAN both need to be connected to the main Source of Power—GOD—*before* attempting to connect to each other. Being connected to GOD supplies both parties with the power they need to love, in spite of any other deficiencies.

> Being plugged into GOD gives You all the love You need so that any other extensions become secondary sources of love.

Simply put, connections with other people are the icing on the cake.

One sure way to know that You are properly connected to the Source of Power is that the desperate edge will be gone from your program. You will be much more discerning about whom You choose to align yourself with. Your intolerance for nonsense and unfruitful associations will be at an all-time high because you'll already feel complete in and of yourself. This security actually makes You more attractive to those around You and serves as a love magnet of sorts.

Your strong connection to the Love Source will also tend to change the sort of men who are attracted to You, increasing the opportunity for quality hookups instead of cheap, temporary fixes. You and the MAN will operate at full love capacity when you are both attached to GOD. "God is love, and whoever abides in love abides in God, and God abides in him. By this is love perfected with us . . . We love because he first loved us" (1 John 4:16–17, 19 ESV). This Scripture is saying that You do not need the auxiliary attachments in order to *feel* love. They simply make You feel *more* love.

Why do You need this primary connection? Neither You nor the MAN should be each other's sole source of love. In the event that You or the MAN suffers a power loss, both units would be unable to function. Therefore, it is vital for GOD to be the central unit for both of you. When both partners strain under their own power to make love work, they cause fuses to short-circuit and may even break their connection.

A friend told me that her capacity to love her husband on a daily basis was based on her love connection to GOD. When she spends time with God and is in a good place with Him, she has a surplus of love to share with her husband. He doesn't irritate her as readily. She's glad to go the extra mile for him. But the moment her relationship with God runs out of steam, so does her relationship with her husband. Small irritations are magnified. He isn't as cute, and she isn't as loving. The importance of our connection to the GOD part is immeasurable when it comes to keeping love flowing. God makes His power available to anyone who wants to make the ultimate love connection.

Before You Love the MAN, You Must Have Your Priorities in the Right Order

You cannot be plugged into GOD and then behave as if You are not. The connection to GOD will always change the way You function. For this reason, You and the MAN must first love GOD with all your hearts, souls, minds, and strength (see Luke 10:27 ESV). That is, You must be fully engaged with Him. He must be your central Power Source.

Loving GOD completely will give You the capacity to love yourself. Believe me, it will be very hard to love someone else if You don't love yourself first. It is easy to see how someone feels about herself if she can't celebrate and love others. If her self-esteem is low, she will be jealous, covetous, and critical of everyone around her. But if she is comfortable in the skin she is in, celebrating the way God created her, nurturing her God-given gifts and nurturing herself according to the Manufacturer's Manual, she will be generous in her praise of others.

To love yourself, You have to avoid comparing yourself to others. Making comparisons results from our need to be validated by an outside source of love that feeds us security. If we're feeling miserably insecure, the only way to make ourselves feel better is to minimize another person—a temporary and hopeless fix at best. There will always be someone more intelligent, more attractive, more witty, more *something* than You. This is a fight You cannot win!

Remember when You were in school? There was always one person who would look at a pretty girl and say, "She thinks she's cute!" If You were discerning at a young age, You would have heard the envy and pain behind that comment. That girl was definitely cute, and the one who had made the snide remark wished to be as cute as she!

Making comparisons will always highlight everything that we are not, magnifying our shortcomings in the light of someone else's accomplishments. Don't go there. Serious breakdowns in your love flow will result. The Manufacturer has crafted each person differently on purpose, to fulfill a specific task. Each person has different functions but equal value. Indeed, we are "his workmanship, created in Christ Jesus for good works, which God prepared beforehand, that we should walk in them" (Eph. 2:10 ESV).

The GOD who is the main Power Source of love is also the One who created You—"fearfully and wonderfully" (see Psalm 139:14 ESV). He celebrated your creation and called You a good thing perfectly fashioned for love. Therefore, when you love yourself according to His design, you'll be able to love the MAN perfectly in sync with GOD's plan.

Only by being connected to this central unit can YOU tap into the current needed to sustain love. Long after you've exhausted your own supply of power, the GOD part kicks in as a generator, releasing a new surge of power to sustain the relationship. Unwrap this piece and place it in the center of your work area. Do not attempt to replace this part with any other one; no other piece will work.

INSIDER'S LOVE TIP
The GOD piece is the only part that can accommodate countless extensions without shorting out its capacity to love. Do not attempt to extend beyond your personal capacity without being plugged into this piece.

The Heart

The Heart is quite a popular part. Fragile but resilient, it is expensive and in high demand. The undiscerning have been guilty of not recognizing its value and treating it with less care than is required. For this reason, this part has often been damaged, broken, and scarred. Many have lost this piece by giving it to the wrong person. In other cases, it has been thrown to one who was not equipped to catch it, and the owner watched it fall to the ground and shatter on impact.

The danger of exposing this piece to abuse and injury repeatedly is that after repair, it can alter itself to accommodate more abuse and actually become attracted to it. This alteration will not allow the part to operate at its greatest capacity. Understand and know that consistent Heartbreak and abuse are never normal, whether you're in or out of love. They are simply unacceptable—period.

The Heart Part

The Heart Is Driven by Its Beliefs

The Heart is very powerful because it harbors all inclinations for love. The tricky aspect is its connection to the Mind (which we will take a look at later). Suffice it to say that the Heart is intelligent. It is driven by its beliefs. The Manufacturer's Manual says, "For as [a woman] thinks in [her] heart, so is [she]" (Proverbs 23:7 nkjv).

For example, if You believe that you are not worthy of love, the HEART will drive You to behave in ways that repel love, thus convincing You that You were right in your conclusion. But You also need to know that the HEART is deceitful and deceptive unless attached to the GOD piece. God will continually check it to keep it virus-free and in proper condition (see Jer. 17:9–10).

The HEART Needs Continual Recalibration

Even when the HEART is attached to the GOD part, it continually has to be recalibrated to function the way it was originally designed. Your HEART can convince You of many things, right *and* wrong. It is important to keep the Manufacturer's Manual close at hand so You can double-check His direction before following your HEART's inclinations.

Remember that story about Samson and Delilah? (Read Judges 14–16.) Long before Delilah came on the scene, Samson was engaged to another Philistine woman. When his parents confronted him about his choice of women, he replied, "She is right in my eyes" (Judg. 14:3 ESV). He let his uncalibrated HEART and hormones lead the way. Later, his unnamed Philistine fiancée turned out to be all wrong for him and even damaged his career as a judge in Israel.

Talk about causing major drama in his life! But Samson still could not get his fill of Philistine women. He kept gravitating to them because they were his "type" (remember?) until he finally landed in the lap of Delilah. There, Samson took a fateful and historic nap that ultimately cost him everything—including his life. So much for listening to your HEART and taking leave of your rational faculties—and GOD.

The HEART is complex, a multifaceted piece of equipment. Therefore, You need to be aware of all its ins, outs, and intricate workings. And You have to know how to keep it operating smoothly.

Some Rules for Keeping the HEART Running

Keep It Clean

It is important to keep the HEART clean in order for love to flow freely and properly. The HEART is prone to storing things that can clog its system. Unforgiveness, bitterness, jealousy, envy, covetousness, pride, greed, lust, and rebellion can do serious damage to the HEART and harden it to the point that it is rendered dysfunctional or paralyzed. Whatever fills the HEART, rules the HEART.

For example: if the HEART is filled with greed, it will choose to get what it wants by using any means, completely disregarding how others will be affected. One HEART can injure another HEART when it becomes so consumed with something that it focuses only on itself.

Again, Samson's flirtations and run-ins with the Philistines put the entire nation of Israel—which he was supposed to be protecting—in jeopardy (see Judg. 15:9–10). Not once did he stop to consider what his temper tantrums would cost others, because he was so focused on what *he* wanted. Therefore, make sure YOU diligently guard your HEART against clutter, viruses and trash. What YOU stow there will affect every facet of your life and determine the health of all of your associations, whether they flourish or fail (see Prov. 4:23).

Rule It

The HEART accumulates many things within its chambers. It can store wisdom, secrets, thoughts, words, truth, imaginations, and lies. Because of its ability to store, it can impact and control the words, as well as the actions, of its host (see Matt. 12:35). Keeping this in mind, YOU need to rule your HEART and prevent it from running amuck.

When filled with the wrong things, the HEART can be rash, troubled, sick if its hopes are denied, faint when overcome with fear or doubt, or uplifted in haughtiness and arrogance. All of these things can jam your circuits, causing the HEART to lock and disengage from others or, worse, to crash and lose all positive data that was stored in its system.

The HEART can actually overheat if overcome with a concern or longing for a person. It can also be cut to the core with conviction when it remains tender, and it can be quick to repent. It can be enlarged with fear or passion or be glad when its desires are fulfilled. It can be steered toward an object or person by the Manufacturer or be solidly set on something or someone.

The HEART can be pliable, loving, and upright. Depending on what it is subjected to, it can serve You well for years to come, or it can be so overcome that You experience a "HEART attack" and fail to function. It may fail to connect to other vital parts, preventing love from running according to design.

How do You make sure your HEART is in prime condition for love? By searching it on a regular basis and purging it of all viruses. You'll need to do some self-examination. I call it *owning your stuff and throwing the trash out*. This practice is necessary in order for two hearts to connect properly.

> When the HEART is functioning at top capacity, it selflessly pours itself out for the benefit of the beloved. It imitates GOD, who is always operating at the peak of lovingkindness.

A well-running HEART considers the needs of the MAN above its own and is ready to exchange life for life once it establishes a permanent connection. There is no greater manifestation of love than this (see John 15:13).

You will either draw the MAN's HEART to You or repel it, depending on how he feels when he is near You. We will discuss this in greater detail in the Assembly section. In the meantime, let's just say that what effect You have on the HEART of the MAN is entirely up to You.

Maintain the HEART'*s Connection to* GOD

Again, your HEART must be connected to the GOD part to function properly. The loss of this connection can occur subtly over time, so YOU will need the help of a HEART specialist to keep all of its inner workings clean and in prime working order.

A HEART specialist, the Master Technician (Holy Spirit) is always available through Tech Support. (YOU can find the contact information in the back of this manual.) Once contacted, the Master Technician will conduct a thorough search of the HEART, report the findings to GOD, and make suggestions to fix what He found (see Rom. 8:27). He will keep watch for any issues that might interfere with the HEART's all-important connection to the Power Source.

Search, repair, and connection accomplished, the HEART is then up and running and ready for love.

Watch It

Please keep in mind that the HEART can be fickle. It can choose to be faithful or unfaithful and requires your constant supervision. If your HEART runs low on its supply of wisdom, YOU must either ask God (see James 1:5) or ask those whose HEARTS are functioning properly for recommendations on how to adjust it.

INSIDER'S LOVE TIP
The HEART is a part that must be used. It will atrophy or harden if allowed to lay dormant for long stretches of time. If your HEART is hard, YOU won't be ready to connect with the MAN when the opportunity comes.

The Soul

The SOUL part is extremely important. It is a central part of your internal hard drive and must be connected to the GOD part in order to function before it can be connected to another soul effectively. In the love equation, YOU will find that two SOULS are necessary for optimum loving.

Do a thorough check of your SOUL before attempting to engage it to another. A SOUL should be whole before it joins another. Two systems will effectively connect and become one if all their parts are working. If your SOUL is fractured or missing parts, it will detract from the other SOUL and deplete its power. This is called *sucking the life out of the MAN*.

The SOUL is the essence of a person. Your SOUL inhabits your body, but the SOUL is a tricky piece, as it is not mortal in nature. It can be wounded, yes, but it never actually dies. It can, however, experience *spiritual* death, which is separation from God. Therefore, YOU need to handle it with care so that it doesn't incur damage you'll have to live with throughout eternity.

Aspects of the SOUL Part

The SOUL Can Be a Fickle Conduit

Many are interested in this part because it can be both good and evil. Indeed, the SOUL is susceptible to outside influences that can affect its internal mechanism. You've watched the news and heard about sinister murderers from their neighbors. The neighbors all seem to say the same thing: "But he was such a nice guy, quiet and unassuming. I couldn't imagine him hurting a fly." Yeah, right! Later in the news broadcast, You realize that the abuse this person endured as a child or the humiliation he suffered when a boss fired him has now pushed him over the edge. The Soul's true workings aren't always clear at first glance.

Think about someone You dated who made You unhappy. He seemed nice enough when You first started seeing each other, but deeper into the relationship You thought, *Who is this person? And what has he done to the nice person I met?* Later You discovered that guy was "punishing" You because of one of his past soured relationships. This kind of behavior is what I'm talking about.

The Soul Is Easily Influenced

The Soul is affected by its environment, other people, and anything that affects the senses, such as sights, sounds, textures, smells, and tastes. The Soul can have deep desires or overwhelming lusts. It can hunger for things in the natural as well as the spiritual, grow weary, become vexed, and grieve to such a degree that it affects the operation of the whole mechanism (your physical body, as well as your life). Your life and even your finances line up with the condition of your Soul.

The Soul Needs Maintenance

The Soul must be maintained in order for it to function at its best, whether it is engaged to another Soul or not. It must be attached to God because it literally draws all of its power from this connection alone.

The initial breath with which God fueled the Soul must be renewed on a regular basis—that is, daily—for the Soul to continue functioning at peak performance. Only the God piece can restore the Soul when it suffers from wear and tear.

As with all the other parts, the SOUL draws its fuel from GOD. It can run only so long on its own before needing to refuel. Those who attempt to run on their own steam usually end up malfunctioning and needing technical support in order to get back up and running. Therefore, YOU need to stay in continual contact with the GOD piece to keep the SOUL operating. Perhaps this is why the psalmist compared longing after the presence of God to thirsting for water (see Ps. 42:1–2).

Think about it. If Jesus, the Son of God, God Incarnate, had to steal away first thing in the morning and in the evening to pray, meditate, and consult with His heavenly Father, how much more does a little ole human like You or me need to do the same? We have to draw energy from a source that is greater than ourselves. God is more than willing to fill our cups to overflowing, not only with wisdom and strength but also with all the love we need to carry us through the day (see Eph. 3:19). Morning and evening pit stops are crucial to the well-being of the SOUL.

The Temptations of the SOUL

Warning: the SOUL can be drawn into being inappropriately sensual, relying on fleshly pleasures for power instead of the real and unfailing Power Source. For example, a sensual SOUL seeks forms of outward stimulation to satisfy inner cravings. A SOUL really lacking love might become gluttonous or addicted, behave lasciviously, or compulsively consume substances or possessions (see Eph. 4:19). The sensual SOUL hardens the HEART and overindulges in things that overpower your ability to make sound choices—while leaving YOU still hungering for love.

The sensual SOUL is trapped in deep bondage with no hope of escape except deliverance from its Creator. YOU can escape only after YOU make a clear resolution to abandon all that is worthless in exchange for only those things that can prosper the SOUL. Only when all the parts are working and aligned properly can the love unit build itself up to function in perfected love (see Eph. 4:16).

It's amazing: we can actually get caught up in going from obsession to obsession. We can go from food to sex to shopping to gambling and then back to food. We keep trying to fill the void—to distract ourselves from our painful hunger for love—with whatever we find. Anything for a moment of comfort, no matter how temporary it is.

We've been led astray by an "If it feels good, do it" culture that never considers the outcome of its actions: the weight gain, the financial devastation, the messed-up relationships, the spiritual bankruptcy.

I don't know about You, but I can tell when I'm on a roll. I throw caution to the wind and begin to consume everything that I know is not good for me. Chocolate! I don't even like it, but I'll eat one candy bar after another. When I finally realize I'm out of control, I stop and ponder something from the Manufacturer's Manual: "Why do you spend money for what is not bread, And your wages for what does not satisfy? Listen carefully to Me, and eat what is good, And let your soul delight itself in abundance" (Isa. 55:2 NKJV).

There is a wealth I can enjoy that is not material. There is an abundance I can enjoy that is not physical. If I can only get beyond my Soul hunger! The Soul was designed to be more sensitive to the wishes of its Manufacturer. When properly configured, it hungers and thirsts for right standing and alignment with the Manufacturer above all other things.

When I have access to the Holy Spirit of God—at all times and in all circumstances—there is no excuse for my dissatisfaction. And when my Soul needs a tune-up, the Manufacturer is right there.

The Soul Tune-Up

At times, the Soul may become overwhelmed by its attachments or surrounding stimuli. If this occurs, You can tune up (restore and refresh) the Soul through a couple of different means. If You fail to correct the problem, your Soul can become totally consumed by its surrounding components. In other words, You can so totally stress yourself out that You become no good for anyone, including yourself. You couldn't make a good decision if your life depended on it.

When you're pulled in all directions, it is difficult to focus on what is truly important—and the important things will inevitably suffer. In effect, You will hinder your capacity to love and greatly reduce your power to maintain healthy and fruitful relationships. If this happens, forget about connecting your SOUL or HEART to another. You'll have nothing to give and be unable to receive. A starved or broken SOUL weakens the heart and makes it sick; the affected unit will not be able to fully commit its energy to any one thing or person. It just doesn't have the juice.

Here are a couple of remedies:

1. Fasting

When I say to use fasting as a way to refresh your SOUL, I don't necessarily mean a food fast, though this is an option to defragment your system. Once, when I found myself continually making wrong choices about men, I declared a MAN fast, a time when I refused to consider another dating prospect or develop a new emotional attachment. I needed to stop and figure out exactly where I had been veering off course.

The MAN fast—taking time out to deal with myself—revealed a host of insights. First, I was attracted to the wrong kind of men. Sad but true: I enjoyed a little trash mixed in with my class. But it was that little bit of trash that ended up causing major problems!

I also discovered that my motivations for finding love were all wrong. Small wonder I gravitated to men who supplied all the wrong things. But in my mind, it was all their fault when I did not get what I really *needed,* versus *wanted,* from them. I found myself frustrated and slowly becoming more and more jaded in my approach to love. I was one messed-up chick!

Not only were my poor choices affecting my love life, but they were also taking a toll on my work and every other significant area of my life. Troubleshooting (reestablishing clear vision) was crucial to rejuvenating my SOUL—solving myself so that I could move past the place where I kept getting stuck.

To me, fasting is simply giving ourselves a rest from whatever is clouding our clear vision. Sometimes we're clogged with food. It makes us sluggish. All the blood has left the brain to deal with what's in the stomach, leaving us at a serious disadvantage. (Do not, however, undertake any kind of dietary fast without first consulting your doctor.)

A subtle deception can keep the owner unaware that her SOUL has been burdened by worldly accolades, monetary rewards, a heap of achievements, and anything else that can tickle the flesh. The SOUL, You see, has one main function: to be a lover and worshiper of God. The SOUL should be so well connected to the GOD piece that it functions at a high level of harmony and victory within the love unit. It should actually manifest the glory and power of the GOD part (see Rom. 15:6).

2. Restoration from God

In times of trial, the SOUL needs encouragement to stay on course. The psalmist would say to himself, "Why are you cast down O my soul, and why are you in turmoil within me? Hope in God" (Psalm 42:11 ESV). He let it all hang out with God. He let God know exactly what was on his mind and in his heart, including the pain he was in and how shocked he was by the deception of his friends. You name it, the psalmist said it to God and then waited for God to encourage, guide, or help him. He had no problem letting God know that some things were just beyond his ability to manage; he was never hesitant to let God know the state of his soul.

If not recharged or cleaned out from time to time, the SOUL can grow faint or melt down under stress. When You begin to tune up the tired SOUL, the Manufacturer restores it to its normal functioning.

Sometimes the Manufacturer waits until You praise Him to restore the SOUL. Praising Him opens valves and releases a wellspring of refreshment that energizes the SOUL and empowers it to love to a greater degree than ever before (see Psalm 36:8–9).

When the SOUL is in mint condition, it is not ruled by outward stimuli. It has desires but does not allow its desires to master it. It functions in a regulated fashion and rejoices in the productivity that comes from operating according to its original design. This fulfillment of purpose empowers the SOUL to love on a deeper level than a SOUL that chooses to follow its own nature instead of aligning itself with the Manufacturer's Manual for living and loving.

A properly kept SOUL is fully compliant with the primary intent of the Manufacturer, which is key to making love work. Your pure and powerful SOUL will attract another pure and powerful SOUL. When engaged, there's no limit to what the synergy of two SOULs can produce. Output that effects positive and lasting change in the lives of all surrounding extensions is the greatest fruit of love, and it is what pleases the Manufacturer most. It is living proof that His creation is a "good thing."

INSIDER'S LOVE TIP
Although it may seem as if your SOUL is no longer your own when joined to another, remember that the Manufacturer is very possessive of this specific part. He has made it known that all SOULs belong to Him.

The Mind

I t's said that if You free your mind, the rest will follow. Nothing could be truer. The Mind runs everything, including the Heart. (This is why I stated earlier that the Heart and the Mind are connected in this mechanism called love.) The Mind is the hard drive in the center of the love unit. It stores all data from your past experiences, conversations, and observations and can greatly influence decisions.

Here's how it works: the Mind convinces the Heart of many things that then move from mere impulses (thoughts) to actual functions (audible words and physical actions), which can be good, not so good, or downright bad. You see, the Mind is the center of your decision making. It tells the rest of You, including the Heart and Soul, how You should feel about any given person, thing, or situation.

When You are operating properly, your emotions *follow* your thoughts. Unfortunately, many feel first and think later—with horrendous results. How many relationships have been short-circuited and destroyed because of this malfunction?!

How the Mind Makes Love Work

Making love work involves not only training yourself to think first, feel later—to keep the Mind and not the Heart in control of your actions—but also disciplining your thought life to work *for* You and not *against* You. I can't count the times I've wished I could snatch back words that spurted from my lips before I had thought them through properly. After I had wounded someone, damage control was very difficult. Small wonder God gave us two ears and only one mouth!

Perhaps we should take the hint to listen more than we speak—which the Manufacturer's Manual actually instructs: "Let every person be quick to hear, slow to speak, slow to anger" (James 1:19 ESV). When we've got it all together and our parts are operating in the proper order, life can be a beautiful thing and our relationships even better than what we've imagined.

Your thoughts determine your decisions and your decisions determine your destiny—including whether or not YOU make love work. YOU have to get a grip on your MIND and put it in check.

Strategies for Optimum Performance

"Cast Down" Bad Thoughts
The Manufacturer suggests in the Manual that we rein in our MINDS by "casting down imaginations, and every high thing that is exalted" (2 Cor. 10:5 ASV)—and drowns out the voice of the Creator. If we can't hear Him, we can't obey Him, and we can't enjoy love as He designed it. The MIND, when corrupted by outside influences, is drawn toward carnal (or unspiritual) thoughts driven by popular opinion or pressing desires. These thoughts are deceptive: they feel good now but usually reap terrible results later.

Carnal corrosion of the MIND leads YOU away from thinking about things that are pure, lovely, virtuous, and praiseworthy. When worldly grit enters the workings of the MIND, it begins to scrape against the GOD part and suggests that YOU think of yourself first—what you want and what YOU need. It tells YOU to assume the worst: "Trust no one. Vulnerability is a crock that only gets YOU in trouble." The carnally controlled MIND stores animosity against the Manufacturer and all that He stands for. It insists on its own way, refuses to work according to the Manufacturer's design (see Rom. 8:7), and leads many to devastation.

Call Up Good Thoughts

You must discipline the Mind to reflect and act on the thoughts and intents of the Manufacturer. Realize how much power You have over your Mind and reel it in. You get to decide what your Mind dwells on. May I recommend that choosing to meditate on the instructions found in the Manufacturer's Manual is a great place to start? As You ponder His thoughts, they will become your thoughts; new thoughts give birth to new actions, and consistent actions result in habits. Those habits shape our character, and our character has an immediate impact on our destiny.

We're talking about your entire life here! Let your life "be transformed by the renewing of your mind" (Rom. 12:2 NIV). Renewing your Mind will lead to making love work! On that note, down with stinkin' thinkin' and up with divine design!

Calling up good thoughts might mean being more selective about what You set before your eyes, what You listen to, and what conversations You take part in. All these things can easily become corrosive grit.

I don't know about You, but after watching something like *Desperate Housewives*, I always feel a little . . . desperate. I know that what I see is what I will begin to believe. The Mind is yet another mechanism capable of focusing on and passing along both good and bad. Therefore, carefully select what you absorb.

As your Mind melds with the Manufacturer's, You will be better able to become one Mind with the Man you are blessed to connect to at some point. He, after all, will also be focused on his Manufacturer. God's ultimate plan is to put two Hearts, Minds, and Souls together in such a way that they become perfectly aligned as one. Operating as a solid unit, such a pair will find nothing impossible to achieve—including lifelong, satisfying, contagious, well-working love!

The Enemy

You need to be aware at this point in the manual that the Manufacturer is constantly warding off a hostile takeover of You and the MAN—via your HEARTS, MINDS, and SOULS—by another company. Satan, LLC (short for Low-Life Counterfeiter), manufactures a remarkable imitation of love.

The loathsome president of this company is dead-set against the Manufacturer's design for love. In his bid to take over, this counterfeiter has released his own ad campaign to tout his much cheaper brand, along with free samples for anyone interested in experiencing immediate gratification (with lasting consequences hidden in the fine print). Satan attempts to influence the HEARTS, MINDS, and SOULS of good people to make them believe that they can achieve love faster if they assemble it his way.

Don't believe the hype. Herein lies the battle for the MIND. We are assaulted daily by movies, reality shows, bachelors and bachelorettes, elimiDates, deceptive thoughts on how to get the guy, and theories on the importance of chemistry and premature intimacy. Such things confuse and dull the MIND's sharp instruments. This problem makes it hard for YOU to discern the right way to implement and get the life YOU want and the love YOU need.

Music also does a subtle come-hither dance with our psyche, luring us to lower our guard and go with the flow, feel the chemistry, get caught up in the moment. Don't think, just do it. Don't think, just feel it. Don't think . . . don't think . . . don't think . . . until YOU hit the wall and come to the painful discovery that your HEART, MIND, and SOUL have been abused, fallen into misuse, and now require repair.

Yes, Satan, LLC, tells YOU to feel now and think later by offering YOU tantalizing treats that he knows will stimulate all of your appetites—the covetousness of the eyes, the lust of the flesh, and the pride of life (see 1 John 2:16). After all, he appeals, "not only are YOU worth it—YOU owe it to yourself!"

But the Master Manufacturer furnishes YOU with the ability to do a virus scan against all things hostile to His brand of love, empowering YOU to delete all negative input, people, or actions from your love connection. YOU will then be able to store and file all incoming thoughts in the appropriate order, which prepares You to operate smoothly and produce the results You want in your relationship as well as your life.

Making Sure the MIND Is in Gear

Meld Your MIND with His

The Manufacturer wants You to be in your right MIND and in harmony with your other parts so You can be free to experience love as He designed it. The only way to achieve this is to allow His MIND to be in You.

How can GOD's MIND be in You? Again, it is important to get rid of all thoughts that do not correspond with the Manufacturer's Manual. Choose to control your thought life by downloading His words into your system, thereby overriding any self-defeating thoughts and habits that are not Manufacturer-friendly (see 2 Cor. 10:5). Internalizing His words will increase wisdom (keep the sharp parts sharp and finely tuned) and get rid of self-defeating thoughts and habits (destroy any corrosive influences) that could deter You from making love work (operate fully) in your life.

For example, according to the Manufacturer's Manual, You are a good thing. You are desirable and beautiful. You are downright lovable!

If You meld your MIND with GOD's in this area, You will walk with a confidence that attracts love to You. You will not compromise on the things that are important to You and ultimately get what You expect because everything about You will say You refuse to take anything less. This attitude prompts the one who truly loves You to step up to the plate.

Dedicate Your MIND to the Manufacturer's Use

In order for the MIND to work at its peak, it must be focused on one thing. It is important that it not fluctuate by trusting the Manufacturer one day and then listening to dangerous influences the next. Take it from someone who knows the dangers of doing your own thing: it's just not worth it! Every time I've grown impatient and failed to trust the

Manufacturer's schedule for love, I've settled for relationships that did more to damage than enhance my life or nurture my heart. Instead of getting the love I wanted, I found myself in need of restoration.

Not focusing on the Manufacturer's Manual will serve only to confuse all circuits and cut off the flow of power to all the parts that need it. MIND function will come to a screeching halt. Don't expect to gain anything if You are double-minded. The MIND must remain fully convinced of the Manufacturer's ability to deliver its expectations. Once it is assured of His ability, it is then free to align itself with the right MAN's MIND, gaining the greatest measure of success with every connection.

Warning: avoid shaking the MIND, as the contents can be damaged or broken. Please refer to the Troubleshooting section of this guide if this has occurred. Cleaning and maintenance will be required to eliminate all thought fragments not conducive to releasing positive power. Realigning all circuits will be necessary to record the proper information and data needed to produce optimum function.

Don't Blame the MIND

One last note: The MIND has long gotten a bad rap for harboring guilt and causing confusion that can sometimes keep the unit from loving as it should. People have spent countless dollars trying to convince the MIND not to feel responsible for things that seem to be deeply imbedded in the internal programming. High therapist bills, anyone?

But guilt is not a function of the MIND. It is a function of the spirit, so it can be solved only by the spirit. I'm not slamming therapists. They are needed and do a lot of good. But I would consider seeking different counsel if a therapist is using methods that work only to sedate, medicate, or rationalize guilt.

I battled severe guilt after the death of my boyfriend. After we had a horrendous disagreement, he decided to take a vacation to cool off. While on that vacation, he was shot and killed. Now, it was not my fault that he was killed. I did not control his decisions or the decisions of those around him. I did, however, contribute to the decision that led to other decisions that eventually led to the end of his life. I needed to own this truth before I could be free of the lingering guilt that was threatening to paralyze me and keep me from ever loving again.

It wasn't until I stopped grappling with whose fault it was or wasn't and instead cried out to the Lord for mercy (Praise God that the Manufacturer has made this feature available to everyone!) that condemnation lifted from me. I was finally able to put the whole ordeal, along with all my regrets and guilt, to rest. The Manufacturer is always available to discuss and correct (see Isa. 1:18).

I know firsthand that to get rid of this pesky but debilitating virus called guilt, You must make sure You are connected to the main Conduit of Forgiveness (Jesus). This connection will override and actually erase all past mistakes and guilt from your personal file, freeing You to function as the Manufacturer originally intended.

Now that You understand that the MIND will be the main drive when it comes to love, take this part and install it next to the GOD and HEART parts to ensure proper assembly.

INSIDER'S LOVE TIP
Your capacity to give and receive love will only be as great as what You believe about yourself and about love.

STRENGTH

S TRENGTH, though seemingly the least glamorous of all the parts, should not be underestimated. The longevity of love's function will be highly dependent on STRENGTH—not feelings, not thoughts, not the opinions of others or all the counseling in the world. What will make love work and last is your commitment, and that will require STRENGTH.

Recently I watched an excerpt from a movie called *Room Ten*. A husband, watching his dying wife, was explaining to the attending nurse the reason their marriage had lasted so many years. He said there was nothing magical about love lasting; it had nothing to do with feelings, and sometimes he and his wife didn't even like each other. But his wife had taught him, no matter how he felt, not to leave the room. That staying power is a sign of STRENGTH.

STRENGTH Is Tough and Vital

There is nothing warm and fuzzy about STRENGTH. It is hard, and it must remain conditioned and ready to operate when all else fails. This part supports all the other parts.

STRENGTH is something YOU decide to use. It must be exercised. Discipline builds STRENGTH. So does letting your partner stretch you beyond your comfort zone emotionally, mentally, spiritually, and physically; persisting through trials and differences; and even allowing yourself to be humbled and broken by what You choose to go through with your partner. All of these experiences make You stronger.

To give up at the first sign of difficulty or irritation does nothing to build the sorely needed element of STRENGTH. STRENGTH inevitably nurtures the endurance that is necessary to sustain love long-term.

If You allow STRENGTH to dry up, it can fail, causing love to stall and eventually break down. Though the STRENGTH part seems capable of enduring more wear and tear than the others, it is susceptible to corruption. When corrupted, STRENGTH drains all the supporting parts and shuts down the HEART and MIND. And then, my friend, it's all over but the shouting (or should I say the alimony settlement?).

Take note, however, that love's failure does not comply with the Manufacturer's design (see 1 Chron. 16:34). He created love to last, to endure the rough patches, to grow and flourish from the heat of trial and tears of disappointment. Love was designed to withstand all external elements and internal meltdowns, emerging victorious in spite of negative currents, shorts, and outages. Love can triumph if STRENGTH is in place.

Are You Strong Enough to Be Weak?

The STRENGTH part actually needs a vulnerable outlet to function at full capacity. Isn't that deep? You need to be strong to be vulnerable and vulnerable to be strong. I once protected myself right out of a relationship because I was too afraid of anticipated pain. I wasn't open, and I blew the whole thing. Can I get a witness?

The bottom line is that we have to be completely dependent on the GOD part for power and be willing to admit our fears and weaknesses (see Phil. 4:13). This dependence and admission can be difficult for those who get pride jammed in their circuits. My suggestion? Get over yourself. Insufficiency is a common trait among all people.

If You refuse to acknowledge that You cannot process love alone, You can get caught in a cross fire of conflicting wills and blow a fuse.

If You and the Man are "faking it until you make it," the two of you will never stay together!

> It is only when You and the Man admit your own weakness that the Manufacturer can supplement your power source with additional Strength.

You will need to repeat this procedure to increase strength in your relationship. Hashing out the issues tightens the bond between You. You really can't have a solid bond until You've been through something together. It is from overcoming and sharing secrets that loyalty and love grow and begin to engage.

What Strength Needs to Function

In order for Strength to function properly, it must have extensions of joy, peace, and confidence.

Joy
This isn't just any joy but a specific brand generated by the Manufacturer Himself (see Neh. 8:10). His joy actually infuses the system with extra measures of strength that confounds even the employees of Satan, LLC. Lucifer and his minions cannot override this device in spite of their sophisticated attempts to do so.

Peace
When Strength is blindsided by Satan's loud and overwhelming campaigns, the Manufacturer orders the part off the market and into solitude. In a quiet place, the Strength piece is able to restore itself to its factory settings. It is only in this solitude that the words of the Manufacturer can reinstate proper order to its system (see Isa. 30:15).

If your STRENGTH has failed, get quiet. Be confident that God
has you covered, and recover from whatever is sapping your energy
and keeping You from doing the work it takes to progress in the
relationship.

Make sense? You can't problem-solve effectively or look at your
partner or potential mate objectively if you're running around with
your hair on fire.

So sit for a spell, take your shoes off, shut out all outside influences,
and reconnect with the Manufacturer. Allow His still, small voice to
give You direction on what to do next. Knowing He is with You gives
You confidence and courage, strengthening You to make love work.

Confidence

Once You see that the Manufacturer can and will sustain the love
You want to secure, your STRENGTH part is back in place and fully
operational. You will be able to weather the storm of any conflict,
and confidence will flourish.

The beauty of the STRENGTH part is that it draws others to You.
They want to siphon assurance and stability from You. Sharing your
strength produces gladness and an ability to laugh at trouble. Because You are confident, You now anticipate the Manufacturer's
intervention if the power needed to make love work exceeds the
capacity of the parts engaged—in other words, if your STRENGTH
begins to fail.

STRENGTH Is Power under Control

When operating at full power, STRENGTH does not yield to pressure
or break under rejection, false accusations, or any other external
afflictions. The STRENGTH part makes You strong enough to die to
your own demands in order to pursue peace. STRENGTH is disciplined
to the point of meekness, which is merely power under control. It
truly requires more STRENGTH to refrain from demanding your own
way when You know You could have it.

Think of Jesus hanging on the cross, and consider the fact that He had angels at His disposal to come to His aid, but He chose to give His life instead. That is deep! It takes great strength not to ego trip, especially when You have the goods to back it up. Restraining oneself allows humility and meekness to operate at their finest.

Though STRENGTH could steer the entire machine, it does not, because it considers the needs of the other parts above its own. This piece is resilient because it has mastered the art of flexibility and discernment. It looks beyond the faults of the other parts, sees the needs and compensates for them, thereby covering more vulnerable pieces with itself.

INSIDER'S LOVE TIP
Keep in mind that after the first flushes of new discovery, excitement, and passion wear off, it is STRENGTH that sustains love for the long haul.

Again, this part is sometimes overlooked because of its quiet operation, but it is a vital part of what it takes to make love work. Keep this part close to You. You will be amazed by how many times you need it.

2

Assembly

"But in fact God has arranged the parts in the body, every one of them, just as he wanted them to be. If they were all one part, where would the body be? As it is, there are many parts, but one body."

—1 CORINTHIANS 12:18–20

Opening and Examining

C ongratulations! Now that you've gotten acquainted with all the parts needed to operate the awesome machine called love, it's time to determine if the MAN you're considering is all YOU hope. Now YOU are ready to begin the most incredible journey YOU can imagine.

Though there are some dos and don'ts when it comes to love, YOU will also find a lot of unpredictability because no two parts are the same beyond their basic wiring. Each comes complete with its own set of unique characteristics and quirks. YOU are like no one else. Neither is the MAN. Therefore, YOU must be open to the subtleties of this complex machine known as love. As we've already noted, the only part that remains exactly the same is the GOD piece. All the other parts are capable of changing shape and even altering their functions, taking a longer or shorter time to line up with the Manufacturer's instructions on how to function in the love unit. So YOU must utilize discernment and grace as YOU begin Assembly.

Discern the Quality of the MAN: Be Open

We must now focus on the MAN part, for it is most critical to how love will work. It is crucial to open and examine the MAN carefully before aligning yourself with him. Once engaged, YOU and the MAN will find it hard to separate.

In order for love to function at its best, YOU and the MAN must be open. As I mentioned earlier, you cannot insist on what the MAN looks like. Instead, have a clear vision of what you would like your love *relationship* to look like. Your choice of MAN may be different from the choices YOU made in the past, because now YOU will base your choice on function, not outward appearance. Remember Proverbs 31:30: "Charm is deceitful, and beauty is vain" (ESV).

Choosing someone according to function aligns with the Manufacturer's policy, which I described earlier, of looking at the heart even though man tends to be moved by outward appearances (see 1 Sam. 16:7). Keep in mind that looks can be deceiving. Your mother said "You can't judge a book by its cover" for a reason!

Some of the most gorgeous men I've dated eventually revealed that they were only pretty houses with no one home or, even worse, less-than-desirable interiors. Some partners are beautiful on the outside, but inwardly their wiring is a mess and they are highly dysfunctional.

I am continually fascinated by those I interview who have been successful at making love work. The report is often the same: "I would never have expected to fall in love with him [or her]. He [or she] was just not my type."

This idea reaches all the way back to biblical times. Boaz was actually surprised to find Ruth at his feet, asking him to be her redeemer. (I do not recommend YOU try this at home or anywhere else in the present day—it was a cultural thing.) He'd kind of figured she'd go for a younger, cuter model. (Read more about Ruth and Boaz in the Manufacturer's Manual, the book of Ruth.)

Ruth, however, had the right idea. She was looking for kindness and security, and that is what she got with Boaz. He was wealthy and may have been easy on the eyes, but who really knows? All we know is that she ended up with a man who took care of her and their family.

Let's face it, how many times have YOU walked down the street or sat in a restaurant, observed a couple, and wondered to yourself, *How did those two end up together?!* This is the mystery of love but also a revelation that everyone will agree on: love does not recognize types.

The Fallout: Failed Relationships

For those who insist on engaging only with partners they consider their type, their configuration might work momentarily but usually cannot be maintained for any great length of time. Sparks can fly when two incompatible people initially plug in—but that's not a good thing! This pair will be unable to access STRENGTH to stay the course.

If instead we take the time to open and examine a MAN, we get to find out what he's really made of. Are his inner workings solid or substandard? Is he a good investment for the long haul or just a pretty ornament for the moment?

Couples usually seem to start off well, don't they? That's why I love what my mentor, P. B. Wilson, says: "Patience is the weapon that forces deceit to reveal itself." She's said a mouthful there! We've seen it happen on various fronts, from politics to personal relationships.

Everyone starts off with good intentions, best foot forward. But get familiar and comfortable with each other and let life hit the fan, let the stress quotient mount, or simply let time do its work, and that's when You see the real deal, raw and naked. The personality that was hidden from You before comes to the forefront in all its glory. Sometimes that can be a hair-raising picture!

The Nonnegotiables

"But," You may be saying, "no one is perfect." True. So should You have standards? Indeed You should, because these standards affect *your* compatibility and your ability to sustain a long-term relationship. In order for the love connection to be secure, both parts—You and the MAN—must operate from the same platform. Therefore, there should be some nonnegotiables about any MAN You consider connecting to.

1. He Must Be Plugged into GOD
First, he should be plugged into the GOD piece, powerfully engaged and passionately interacting in a way that it is giving off positive output.

This connection should be something a lot deeper than a MAN's knowing *about* Jesus or simply being "spiritual."

The MAN You are considering should be involved with and accountable to God. (See Ps. 1 in the Manufacturer's Manual for characteristics of a godly man.) The accountability factor is huge; if he won't break the heart of God, he won't break yours, either.

There is a reason that foremost of the Ten Commandments is to love GOD. Jesus added that You should then love your neighbor as yourself. Jesus knew that if You loved God and people enough, You wouldn't lie, cheat, steal from them, or do anything else that would hurt them (see Matt. 22:25–40). Makes sense to me. I think You get the picture. Moving on . . .

2. He Must Be a Working MAN

Second, the MAN should be working. In urban culture, women say they are looking for a BMW—Black MAN Working—but I'm sure this holds true for everyone (see 1 Tim. 5:8). Your potential mate should know and understand his purpose, have a vision for his life, and be actively engaged in pursuing it. The alternative is not pretty, especially when it begins to affect the economic quality of your life (see Prov. 24:33–34).

If You ask a MAN what he wants to do with his life and he says, "I don't know," don't walk—*run!* When Ruth met Boaz, he was in the midst of harvesting his crops. I think their meeting demonstrates a spiritual principle very nicely. She was gleaning, he was harvesting. Both people in the equation need to be producing fruit. Both of you should have something to show for yourselves besides great ideas.

Life costs money, so You can't afford to be so romantic that You don't care what a MAN is going to do for the rest of his life. Believe me, it will eventually affect You and hit You where it hurts, namely your financial security and future. Not that you're marrying for money, but finances do become an important part of the equation, one that can affect your HEART condition over time. There's a reason finances are one of the top three causes of divorce.

3. He Must Have Integrity

Third, the MAN should have integrity. He should be true to what he was designed to do and true to You. There should be no question about his intentions toward You or his ability to deliver what he promises. In other words, he considers your time and your heart when making plans or commitments to You. He does what he says he is going to do. The MAN should have no problem being transparent with and accountable to You. His failure to do so early on gives You a hint of your future: a string of broken promises and bad feelings that build up to one big explosion and major heartbreak. How You begin is how You will end, but on an escalated level. An inch becomes a mile when left untended. Remember that.

4. He Must Have Good Current Relationships

Next, check out the MAN's connections. Let's begin with family. Where a MAN comes from has a lot to do with how he will function in relationships—as they say, "The apple doesn't fall far from the tree."

When David took Bathsheba, the wife of Uriah, and had Uriah killed to cover his misdeed, he spread a spirit of entitlement to his sons that became apparent in shocking ways. Amnon raped his half sister Tamar. Absalom killed Amnon in revenge then tried to take the throne from his father and went as far as to sleep with David's wives on the rooftop of the palace, in full view of everyone. Oh, the drama families can pass on to one another. We see this throughout the Bible. Abraham lied, his son Isaac lied, Isaac's son Jacob was also deceitful . . . see what I mean?

I once had a boyfriend who was quick to take offense anytime I made a suggestion to him. I couldn't understand why he went ballistic at the slightest comment that was contrary to what he might have been thinking. Then I met his mother, and it all made sense. He had tons of unresolved anger toward her that dated back to when he was five years old! He projected her critical attitude onto me. I was just like his mother—or so he believed. This issue caused problems that I knew would not be resolved until he healed. Suffice it to say that because he wouldn't acknowledge his lingering anger as a problem, our relationship did not work. I grew weary of backpedaling in every conversation, and he got tired of being angry.

Families can also share good traits. Jesus was quick to say that He reflected the heart of His Father—that if You saw Him, You literally saw the Father, because they were one and the same (see John 14:9). This concept is usually true of our earthly partners, too. That future husband is going to look just like his father in twenty years and, generally speaking, he will probably operate the same way and value the same things his father does.

So decide if You like what You see. Check out how the MAN relates to his parents, his siblings, and others with whom he has significant relationships. Is there a positive connection?

Remember that all negative links will affect your interaction with this person. You may not be marrying the family, but You will be inheriting their issues. Negative energy will be transferred to You, overwhelming all of your positive output until You or the MAN blows a fuse and chooses to disconnect. In other words, the issues he has with his mama will become issues he has with You. Listen to how siblings talk about your partner, 'cause, honey, they will tell You the truth!

5. He Must Have Good Past Relationships

Though discussion about former love connections is not advised in initial contact (this is called TMI—Too Much Information), You need to pay some attention to a MAN's history to get an idea of how he functions in relationships.

A track record of numerous short-term romantic, platonic, and/or professional relationships could be evidence of faulty wiring that makes your potential love unable to commit long-term. It is important to ask the hard questions early so You can decide if You want to invest in this person. The fallout of a broken heart can be costly.

I once met a man who had a number of children by four different women, which obviously spoke volumes about his character. The ages of these children were not that far apart—as a matter of fact, a few of them overlapped! Not only did this tell me things about him he probably would never have admitted to me, but it also gave me pause for a different reason. If I chose to be in a relationship with him or, even more seriously, chose to marry him I would then have to pay for all of his choices before he met me: namely, seven children!

Each person must make these decisions at her discretion, but seven kids is a mighty high price to pay for companionship if children are not on your priority list—at least it was for me. At the end of the day, You must be able to take off the rose-colored glasses no matter how great all of the attention feels and deal with the cold, hard facts. They'll be staring at You once the honeymoon is over.

6. He Must Have Godly Friends

Make sure that You check out his pals, as they will be extensions of him in your life. Friends reveal a lot about the person You are considering because they can be considered duplicates. Birds of a feather flock together. If You do not like a man's friends, understand that they are displaying something—behaviors, habits, attitudes—he might be hiding from You. That is, his friends may reveal who he is when he is not with You. For this reason, patience and discernment are required when you're trying to find a MAN with whom to make love work.

7. He Must Affect You for Better, Not Worse

A positive bond should empower You and strengthen your connection to the GOD part, as well as to other people, such as friends, family, associates, and coworkers. It should also empower You internally to feel good about yourself, increasing love in your life on all levels.

If the MAN is draining You—causing You to compromise your standards, question your personal value, or be at odds with others to the point of isolation—break this connection! It is unhealthy and will result in lasting damage to your ability to love again. Remember, the market is flooded with other people all seeking the same connection.

For this reason, never settle for parts that are discounted or on sale (they may be easy to get only because they are hiding defects You will not want to deal with!), who sell themselves cheap or seem waaay too available. These parts may be available because they've got nothing else going on in their lives, which means they have nothing to offer You—experientially or materially. You will get what You pay for, and believe me, there is a price attached to love. (We will cover this in the Maintenance section of this guide.)

Why Examination Is So Important

When the Israelites were traveling to the Promised Land with Joshua, they ran into some smooth-talking enemies who wanted to enter into a covenant relationship with them. The scariest part of the story is one little sentence: "So the men took some of their [the enemy's] provisions, but did not ask counsel from the LORD" (Josh. 9:14 ESV). They got in big trouble later, when they discovered that the foreign men were really adversaries, but by that time, they were in too deep and could not back out of the covenant they had made.

You have to ask hard questions not only of a MAN, but also of his friends, family, and, above all, God. If You do not have peace about connecting with someone, save yourself the drama and the trauma that will be yours after You find out he is not the person You thought he was. Sometimes the immediate gratification of what he offers—be it affection, attention, or gifts—will distract You a little from the real point: is this person right for You? Do your homework up front.

Just as one must interview candidates for a job, You should "interview" dating candidates to find out if the MAN is qualified to be a husband. Not every MAN is husband material, just as not every woman is wife material. This matter is one of title versus function; You have to be clear about both to discern if the MAN that sits before You is capable of performing the necessary functions (see Luke 14:28). It is the most difficult job on earth to master—that of being a perfect mate according to the Manufacturer's design.

Now is the time to find out what a MAN wants his life to look like over time. YOU might find that your goals are different. How does he spend money? How does he handle stress? How does he speak to YOU and others? Is he considerate and sensitive to your needs? What is his attitude toward your views, goals, and gifts? Is he a MAN of discipline—faithful to keep his word? What is his reputation like at church, at work, among his family and friends? What is his relationship with God like? What is his sense of community at work and church as well as at home? (And this is the *short* list!)

Make a list of things that are important to YOU, and take the time to get answers to the questions that will matter to YOU after the first sparks have stopped flying. Ultimately, YOU will be responsible for the condition of your HEART, so take care what other parts YOU align it with.

INSIDER'S LOVE TIP

As you open up your partner, choose to be open yourself. As YOU examine your partner, examine yourself. Never demand or expect more than YOU are able to give yourself. Love does not always seem fair, but it is always just, always choosing the greater good over what is convenient.

Configuring

So you've asked the initial hard questions and made your observations. You like what you've heard and seen. Now is the time to become more intentional in your approach to making a working love connection. After You gather all the data on the Man, some configuration must take place to discern compatibility.

This means that, as previously mentioned, You must know yourself and your purpose before You can know if the Man is going to be a good fit. Will the Man be an appropriate partner for your fulfilling the Manufacturer's plan for You? Will You be an appropriate partner for the Man?

If You are unsure of what God made You for, do not attempt to go any further. Understanding your purpose will be crucial to the configuration process.

Blocks to Effective Configuration

Failure to Discern Your Purpose
Purpose is what puts You in position to meet your partner. If You place the cart before the horse, You might misplace your purpose. Hence the common complaint of married women that they've lost their identities in the process of connection. The truth of the matter is that they never established their identities. Once a woman fully understands her purpose, she cannot misplace it unless she chooses to do so in exchange for a relationship with a Man.

When a woman fails to establish her identity, dissatisfaction causes her to say to her partner, "You are not making me happy." This statement, however, is a perversion of truth because in actuality, the woman has made herself unhappy by not functioning according to her original design or purpose—or even taking the time to find out what it is.

This is the point at which most connections run into serious interference or break down altogether. Many former couples report that they "outgrew each other" or "grew apart." In many of these cases, the initial configuration never took place, which left both partners open to more conflict than they were equipped to handle.

Failure to Discern His Purpose

> It is important to realize that what You *initiate* is what You will *generate*.

If You are operating under a Manufacturer's policy that states You cannot fix or return a MAN once You have committed to him, You will be more intentional in your alignment. The MAN should make his needs, aspirations, and standards known in the beginning so that there will be no surprises later—and so should You. It is exceedingly better to know that you've chosen the wrong person *before* You are attached to him.

Failure to Find Agreement

In order for love to work, the two parts—You and the MAN—cannot be polar opposites. I mentioned earlier that You need to be similar at the core but different in function. The power of agreement will make your connection strong.

Janet and Paul, friends of mine, are so much alike that over the years they've even begun to look like each other. On the other hand, a friend of Janet's, Sarah, is in a turbulent marriage. As she and Janet discussed the phenomenon of Janet and Paul's oneness, Sarah asked, "Do you think Justin and I look alike?" Janet replied, "Not at all!" Sarah looked sad and reflected, "I guess when you aren't one, you don't look like one."

Truer words could not be spoken. The objective of any couple should be to live inside each other to the point that their power to overcome obstacles in life increases. Goals must be outlined, as this can be a major source of love failure. If one person wants to be a missionary and the other a socialite, they need to choose partners more in line with their aspirations. YOU should never try to reprogram the MAN (and vice versa), as this will lead only to a lifetime of frustration.

MAN, Meet Woman;
Woman, Meet MAN

A final block to configuration is significant enough that it deserves a whole section: YOU cannot configure if YOU or the MAN has issues about gender roles. Though these roles sometimes appear to conflict, they are complementary in the function of love. We all are aware of John Gray's theory that "men are from Mars and women are from Venus," but keep in mind that though Mars and Venus are different planets, they are part of the same solar system!

Someone once said to me, "Being a woman is hard." I replied, "It is if you're a woman who is trying to be a man." When we step on each other's toes and roles, trouble begins. Though male and female functions seem to be opposite, each has its own part in the love machine—if it is allowed to do what it is supposed to do, according to God's design.

Men and women must agree to allow each other to function in their roles, free from static, so both can perform at their authentic best. In other words, let men be men, and let women rejoice in their femininity for all it's worth.

I once had an interior designer explain the law of room design to me. She used the words "tension and release" in reference to the balance in space and the things placed in a specific area. I think the same holds true for relationships—there must be tension and release. Where two people do the mating dance, the MAN releases the woman to be a woman, and the woman releases the MAN to be a MAN. The chemistry between them then creates this wonderful tension that actually pulls them together as they release each other to be who they are. Wow! That's pretty amazing, huh?

So let's be clear on what we are dealing with lest we get confused by media hype and insinuations. Though both men and women have equally strong roles, God designed them to submit to each other, accommodate each other's weaknesses, and balance their strengths. Let's take a look.

A MAN's Role

The MAN was created as the initiator, protector, and provider and serves the female without overpowering her (see Eph. 5:25). Because the male is the initiator, the female must not pursue the male. Jesus is the prototype for the ultimate Bridegroom. He wooed, pursued, fought for, and died for His bride (that would be us—the church collectively). We don't run after Him; instead, we respond to the love He initiated (see 1 John 4:19).

Ever notice that no one gets married on *The Bachelor* after the season finale? That's because this spiritual principle has been overlooked. What MAN is going to respect any woman who engages herself in full-on pursuit of him, especially in an arena where many other women are also vying for his affection?

This is role reversal at its worst. She has become the hunter and he the game. But wait a minute—he was created to be the hunter! Notice that the only successful union from these reality shows has been from *The Bachelorette*, where the men were in their rightful place, pursuing a lady.

I know it's popular in culture now for women to be independent and prove that they are equal to men by acting like them, but this behavior has consequences. If the woman chooses to be the initiator and happens to win his attention and affections, she will set up a pattern of continually having to push all the MAN's buttons to get reassurance of his love. When the woman is chosen by the MAN, she is able to rest comfortably in their relationship without insecurity, knowing he did the work to claim her hand.

A Woman's Role

The female actually has the easy job in life. She is made to be a receiver, kind of like the one in a stereo system (see Eph. 5:22). The receiver takes the power from what it's plugged into, channels the energy, and outputs beautiful music. Even GOD said (in the book of Genesis) that it is not good for a MAN to function alone. Without a woman, he is missing a piece of himself as well as a vital source of power that he needs to complete his designated assignment or purpose.

A woman empowers a MAN as she receives and submits to his love, just as the church submits to Christ, honoring Him and proving our love for Him through our obedience. A woman makes her MAN feel loved by honoring him and cooperating with him. In the end, she reaps the benefits: a MAN honors her because of how good she makes him feel.

I get this picture of Adam supervising the Garden of Eden, keeping the animals in check and reporting to God about how everything was going. After a while, God decided some creativity was needed—enter Eve, stage left. She brought a whole new energy to the garden, and in no time Adam was head over heels in love with her. I'm sure they were inseparable right up to their little afternoon snack that shaped the destiny of the rest of the world.

And that's when one of the greatest facts about the dynamics of men and women was revealed. The woman comes equipped with the power to influence the MAN, though the MAN has authority to guide the couple as a unit. In some cases, the female's influence can override the authority of the male.

Think about it this way: GOD has all authority, but your HEART can influence YOU to disobey Him. Though He has authority, YOU have freedom of choice. When a woman influences a MAN against the way he is wired, it can short-circuit his power. Simply put, the female can emasculate the male, which then places their connection in danger. Remember that when a woman resorts to the use of male energy, she leaves her MAN with two choices—to abdicate his masculinity or to leave and go where he can continue to output male energy. Both choices usually have disastrous ends.

This is what happened with that famous villainous woman of the Bible, Jezebel (read 1 Kings 21 and 2 Kings 9:30–37). When she didn't feel that Ahab was moving fast enough to get what he wanted, she took over. She challenged him, "Are you king or not?!" and proceeded to run the show as if she were king. Her actions landed them all in a heap of trouble with God that ended in the loss of their kingdom, period.

Jezebel, in particular, met a very ugly end. She was hurled from her palace window, went *splat* in the middle of the street, was over-run by enemies' chariots, and her remains were eaten by dogs.

Ewww. That is a graphic description of how ugly a woman looks when she decides to take on a man's characteristics.

Meanwhile, Ahab rolled over and abdicated completely, took to his bed and became a complete wimp. Though he had no part in Jezebel's dirty work, he was still held accountable for it and suffered an untimely end. Are You getting the picture?

When a woman exerts male energy (by taking over) and a MAN exercises female energy (by submitting to her leadership), serious technical difficulties result.

Choosing to Love Rather Than Coexist

In many cases, You find men and women merely existing together. This will never be enough for either partner; they will always expect to get something more out of the love connection. These unmet expectations will lead to a slow buildup of negative residue in the relationship. When resentment sets in, respect is lost, which is followed by a depletion of desire and the eventual breakdown of the relationship.

To avoid these types of errors, which interrupt the flow of love, each partner must be clear on the importance as well as the benefits of how the other functions. When a MAN and a woman agree to honor each other by celebrating and balancing their differences, they complement each other and discover mutual satisfaction in their relationship.

Now, both parts are free to discuss how they will balance their strengths and weaknesses to create the most powerful working unit. For example, my mother is better at balancing checkbooks and managing finances, while my father is a real fix-it man. They yield to each other's strengths without stepping on each other's toes. They each submit to the other's design. It works for them—'nuff said.

An honest assessment of each other's gifts is necessary to see how you configure according to the Manufacturer's design and distribute tasks between you. Such tasks can range from the mundane (household chores) to the critical (financial planning). The key is for the two of you to agree. But you need to settle this issue of distribution while you are in the initial stages of configuration if you want to make love work.

Remember, people, like parts, are what they are. They've already been formed and wired. Only the Manufacturer can rewire. When people and parts are allowed to be what the Manufacturer designed them to be, they are stronger and have more to give to the relationship. As partners celebrate each other's strengths and balance out their differences, they are able to merge their gifts. They are able to make love work and become a fabulous picture of the Manufacturer's design.

INSIDER'S LOVE TIP
A part will have difficulty functioning only when it attempts to be—or is forced to be—a different part. When this occurs, successful operation is impossible.

Initializing

To initiate the connection and set up properly, You must start with a clean, even surface as well as parts that have been prepared for connection. Lay all the parts in plain view in front of You along with the diagram from the Manufacturer's Manual for love. Might I suggest that You read 1 Corinthians 13, the "love chapter," as well as 1 John 4:7–21? Though love is found throughout the entire Manual, these two sections will give You the main bullet points.

Initializing is the turning point: You are no longer flirting with the idea of connecting. You are taking serious steps toward a decision to join. You are getting to know the Man on deeper and deeper levels. After opening and examining the surface traits of the Man, You must now evaluate his attitudes as well as his interactive skills with You in particular. In the initializing phase, You are seeing if your formats are compatible.

Levels of "Knowing"

There are several levels of getting to know someone. The Manufacturer's Guide makes it clear that this is an important stage in initializing: "Suppose one of you wants to build a tower. Will he not first sit down and estimate the cost to see if he has enough money to complete it? For if he lays the foundation and is not able to finish it, everyone who sees it will ridicule him, saying, 'This fellow began to build and was not able to finish'" (Luke 14:28–30 NIV). Trust me:

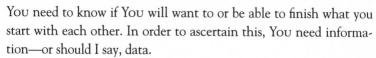
You need to know if You will want to or be able to finish what you start with each other. In order to ascertain this, You need information—or should I say, data.

You need to understand that there are two levels of getting to "know" your partner, as this one area can destroy the entire connection if attempted too early in the sequence of Assembly.

Level 1: Data Gathering

In the first stage of initializing the connection, You accumulate data on character and tendencies and all the facts, stats, and details so You can decide whether your connection would be an effective one. This is the first level of knowing. We talked about this in the *Opening and Examining* section.

Level 2: Transmission or Courtship

Transmission is the crucial stage before merging You and the MAN. Here is where all extraneous matters are addressed and settled in preparation for You and the MAN to determine whether or not to establish a more decisive link.

It is important to know what love looks like before attempting to put it together. In short, love is patient, kind, not jealous or boastful or rude. It does not demand its own way. It is not irritable and keeps no record of when it has been wronged. It is never glad about injustice but rejoices whenever the truth wins out. It never gives up, never loses faith, is always hopeful and endures through every circumstance. It lasts forever. (See 1 Cor. 13.)

Many have attempted to put two hearts together without a working knowledge of what love should look like—with painful results. Others have tried to construct it by imitating images they've seen in the movies only to be disappointed. Love has gotten a bad name from being poorly assembled.

Many have tried to set up two main parts, hoping to create a love connection, only to find that they did not know enough about You or the MAN to make the right match. Both parts inevitably end up going in separate directions, wondering, *What were they thinking?!* about their matchmakers. Blind dates are pretty much just that: shots in the dark with the hope that two people whose singleness makes others uncomfortable will finally put everyone out of their misery. At least that's what many victims of blind dates end up believing.

Most of the confusion comes from what both parties have weathered prior to the current possible hookup. If they have experienced a string of unsuccessful relationships, they will become accustomed to an imitation of love and adapt to these lower quality versions. Though uncomfortable, dysfunctional love will become "normal" to the parties involved, and they will then practice this counterfeit form of relationship until they are forced to be authentic.

Once this wrong perception of love becomes instilled in the MIND, HEART, and SOUL of a person, it affects him or her on every level. This person never pursues love based on the Manufacturer's design because he or she doesn't know what to look for.

In other words, what YOU experience repeatedly as "love" will become what YOU believe is "love." What YOU believe is what YOU will live out. Here is where most women lose it. After repeated rejections, they come to believe that they are worthy only of substandard love and eventually end up in relationships that are far less than what they truly desire. Still, because of low self-esteem, they believe this love is as good as it gets for them.

To prevent dysfunctional love from becoming a habit or your norm, YOU must minimize the bad experiences during courtship by making more informed choices about the MAN YOU invest your heart in. (After all, every investment should create a healthy return.)

Don't Become a Baggage Carrier

I've mentioned this before but want to reiterate it now: it is important to examine your potential mate to make sure he is free and clear of excess appendages (that would be baggage), such as past attachments or even bad programming from former associations. If You do not do this, You as well as the Man may develop an immunity to love as it should be and actually assimilate dysfunction.

Please note that while everyone has some amount of baggage from the journey of life, there are healthy amounts and amounts that are seriously unacceptable. Even the airport charges You extra money if your bags are over a certain weight! Therefore, it is best if the "bag" is not a burden, can be unpacked without drama or great difficulty, and contains items that don't drastically or negatively affect your life.

Carrying too much baggage leads to a cycle of perverted love relationships. Generally speaking, damaged people are attracted to each other because of familiar feelings, even if they are not good ones. Subconsciously, they hope that someone will compensate for their weaknesses. But in most cases, one broken person only enables another to remain broken or deepens the damage already done.

I can cite myself as a good example. I was one of those women constantly attracted to the "bad boy," the one who would never commit. When the relationship went awry, the thrill of the game mingled with the agony of rejection. Finally, I concluded that I was the culprit. *I* was the commitmentphobe who kept gravitating toward those who would not fulfill my true desires.

You couldn't have told me this about myself. I would have argued with You to the bitter end. It wasn't until I took the time to deal with myself and my fears that I became attracted to a different type of Man and no longer tolerated bad behavior. I really clarified what I was looking for and eliminated those who did not fit my outline. I left room for some variation, but the bottom line was nonnegotiable: the Man for me had to have godly character, had to be intentional and committed, and could not subtract from who I was. (See the *Opening and Examining* aspect of Assembly for more details on nonnegotiables.)

Don't make the mistake of allowing another person to minimize who You are with selfishness.

Love is not a selfish machine. It is constructed and programmed to give more than it receives. It is compensated by
the joy that comes from empowering the MAN.

It is in giving that You actually receive. Having a fundamental understanding of what love should look like and how it should function
prepares You and the MAN for a mutually satisfying experience.

Make sure that the person you intend to connect with is wired to
relate in a healthy manner. You should not have to spend the entire
courtship telling your partner how to be kind to You! You train children and influence adults—there is a difference. You should never
be put in the position of being the MAN's mother because he already has
one. So if the basics are not in place and he is getting more out of the
relationship than You are, now is the time to notice and unplug from
the connection—before it's too late.

Your Role in the Courtship

As You and the MAN enter this stage, understand that a woman's job
is simply to be a woman. During courtship, be open, friendly, available, and responsive. Allow the MAN to do the work of pursuing the
relationship—he needs to feel as if he earned his treasure.

Sadly, many a MAN has been ruined by aggressive women doing all the
work. This is not your job. You simply have to let a MAN know where You
are coming from and what makes You feel wanted. This should not be
overdone. Let him know that You enjoy his attention and spending time
with him. Let him know the things he does that make You feel good.

For example, if You say, "Hey, thanks for getting that. It's so good to
know that chivalry is not dead," then he knows that You like it when he
opens the door for you. Not a big deal, but it lets him know what kind
of woman You are without giving him a list of demands. If he *doesn't* get
the door, don't move, and wait for him to get it. If he barges ahead of
You, just sweetly ask, "Can you get that for me?" From there, it is up to

the MAN to take the ball and run with it. If he doesn't, he's revealing something important about himself, and YOU should not ignore it.

If he is spoiled and used to having everything handed to him on a platter, YOU want to know now so YOU can discard this particular MAN. Alignment with him will lead to a slave-like existence for YOU, and the love will flow only one way.

The MAN must be clearly intentional in moving the relationship forward and solidifying the love connection. I know society has tried to program YOU differently—to make YOU the aggressor—but it's faulty programming. Resist it. Your job is to respond to his advances, making him feel wanted and needed and all that wonderful stuff so that he feels encouraged to continue his pursuit of YOU.

Feel free to ask questions, however, so that YOU know whether YOU want to progress. But a warning: do not question him on his intentions prematurely, as this could short-circuit his wooing process. If he feels pressured to respond to questions before he has the answers, YOU may scare him off.

Initially, all the MAN knows is that he is interested in YOU. He does have an internal alert that tells him when he has met "the one," but he usually still takes the time to confirm this by the way the two of you interact.

So when is the right time to ask where the relationship is going? The moment he makes any moves toward intimacy. YOU then have the right to ask because he is asking YOU to share what is precious to YOU with him. Your HEART, your MIND, and your body *are* precious: never give these to someone until he has proven that he honors YOU. (Even then, YOU are responsible for guarding and maintaining your HEART, MIND, and body.)

Tips for a Healthy Courtship

1. *Keep Your Mystery*
During courtship, YOU will tell him (in words and actions) what kind of woman YOU are. YOU are unique, with your own brand of needs

and qualities that appeal to You, and that is a part of what makes You a mystery in his eyes. Your uniqueness is more powerful than You know! Keep just enough mystery to keep him wanting more, but make sure that You don't play games—that is, don't try to manipulate him into doing or not doing things.

For example, sometimes women like to share how badly the last man hurt them, hoping to garner a sympathy vote from their present suitor. This plan could backfire, by drawing attention to something that You don't really want him to consider. Therefore, don't tell him about every relationship you've ever had.

Keep your personal issues and struggles to yourself until he gives You clues that tell You he's ready to hear them. Never give him information that could work against You unless it will directly affect him and your life together should you become a permanent couple. Some things should be kept until You are in love, because *love* is much more understanding than *like*. If You do feel the need to share something deep and murky about your past, leave this up to the prompting of the Manufacturer. Otherwise, remember that it's called a personal life for a reason, and keep it to yourself.

2. Don't Make Him Your Everything

Be authentically yourself, and have a life, activities, and friends beyond the person you're courting. A MAN will always be attracted to a woman who makes him feel wanted but does not make him her oxygen. He knows the difference between desire and desperation. One draws him, and the other makes him flee.

3. Celebrate Your Differences

During this time of getting to know each other, you need to become as acquainted with your differences as with your similarities. If you can learn to celebrate them, your differences will lead to more fulfillment than you can imagine. One of you may be more outgoing and less mindful of details while the other is more laid-back and systematic in his or her thinking. While these traits can be irritants, they can also be great balancers. Both of you have qualities that could make you stronger as individuals when you choose to work as a team. Let your differences — if they're not any of the nonnegotiables (see the *Opening and Examining* section) — bring you closer.

Though the Manufacturer's Manual gives us an outline of what love looks like, the picture becomes clearer as the two connected parts begin to release their power to each other. You will find that though the basic model of a love machine has the same foundational components, each model or couple has its own unique features. This is why initializing is important in order to solidify the engagement of both parts prior to establishing a permanent link. But this is the mystery of love — after all is said and done, two can become one. And that's the only way for love to work.

INSIDER'S LOVE TIP
The secret to the YOU and MAN parts joining together smoothly is found in the ability to celebrate each other's differences. One part's insistence on assimilating the other part's mold and function will cause resistance in coupling.

Merging

I f You have progressed past the initial setup without getting bogged down or overwhelmed by the courtship phase of your relationship—meaning you still both possess mutual attraction and deep "like" for each other and your platforms appear to be compatible—then You are ready to consider entering engagement or "merging" with the MAN.

Let me say again that this step is advisable only if both of you are firmly connected to the GOD part. The GOD part will not only lengthen and strengthen your connection to the MAN; it will also act as a surge protector. Should either You or the MAN suffer from power surges or outages, the GOD part will serve as a buffer, preventing permanent and irreparable damage.

As You move closer to making a permanent commitment, take some time to consider these last recommendations.

Getting Ready to Connect at the Family Level

Different Life Lessons

We've acknowledged that the MAN's relationships with his family members will reveal much to You about how he would relate to You as his wife (and family). I want to add here that You must keep in mind that every person functions according to what he was taught and what he witnessed from the day he was born. If your family relations, traditions, and experiences were vastly different from his, it will be hard to correspond on the same platform, and the quality of your life could be impacted.

One lie begets another, as we see when we trace the hereditary inclinations of Abraham and his son, Isaac. Moved by fear, Abraham resorted to lying about his relationship with his wife, Sarah. "She's my sister, not my wife," he told the Pharoah (see Gen. 20). Fast-forward years later to find Isaac presenting the same lie in reference to his wife, Rachel (see Gen. 26:1–11). His son, Jacob, took deceit to a whole other level that eventually caught up with him and back-fired. By then, he was married and his entire family was affected. Read about it in Gen. 27–30. After merging, You may not have to live with your partner's family, but never be deceived into thinking that familial habits don't come to live at your house and affect your world directly, because they most certainly do.

The Family Name

Another point about families: their reputations precede them and reveal their true character. There's a reason the Manufacturer's Manual says that "a good name is to be more desired than great wealth" (Prov. 22:1 NASB). Your name can create favor or disfavor for you. When You take on the MAN's name, his family's reputation will begin to affect yours. The fact is, your decision to attach yourself to someone, or to someone's family, who is not respected or even liked could mar your stellar reputation and affect your life on many levels.

Please be careful, however, to judge every MAN on his own merit. Don't throw out the baby with the bathwater. If he's a great MAN who has managed to rise above all the madness of his family with consistency, by all means give him a chance.

Regarding names, I must interject here that every trademarked item bears the name of its umbrella company. In marriage, you are creating your own brand that should be trademarked by the two of you shar-ing one name—his name. In the same way, you also share one solid identity.

The MAN feels secure when he functions according to the Manufacturer's design. He is wired to name the woman. This solidifies his identity and reminds him that he is your covering. When the woman keeps her name, the link is always in question. Though he may have agreed to this condition, it becomes a point of spiritual unrest that could render the link unstable.

While the Love Is Flowing, Keep Your Eyes Open

We've taken time to check out the MAN pretty thoroughly, but it's still important to keep watch for anything that might have slipped by You in the courtship days. Now that you're moving toward merging for life, be aware of any flashing warning lights. It's the little things that can cause major disconnection.

At first, You can overlook these "little issues" because of all the electricity flowing between You and the MAN. Though it may feel good, this electricity does distract from issues that will become important should you decide to solidify your connection.

The fact is, what is cute today will be annoying tomorrow. Many have wanted to unplug after living with the other person for some time. They discovered that minor annoyances and disagreements mushroomed into insurmountable conflicts.

Pay attention to all flashing lights: long amounts of time away from You that are vaguely explained or unaccounted for, things said that raise questions You do not ask, any compromises that are waved away, habit changes, signs of moodiness. When in doubt, do not move forward until you've reached a place of peace.

Many who have allowed a rented hall and mailed invitations to keep them from pulling the plug on their nuptials find that the repair bill from counselors, the fees for divorce, and the lasting heartache are far more expensive.

Make Sure He's Professional Grade
If You were on a plane and heard that the pilot had never flown before but was willing to give it a go, You would be off that plane in no time

flat. No way would You fly with someone not qualified to get You to your destination safely. Then why do this when it comes to marriage?

I'm *not* saying You should marry someone who has tried it before. What I *am* saying is that, just as You wouldn't board a plane flown by an unqualified pilot, You shouldn't get engaged to a man who isn't marriage material. Sure, your examination of his character and the courtship should have revealed this fact, but many women, in love with love or at least in love with the idea of a wedding, have chosen to dismiss this vital element.

Yes, even at this advanced stage, You may be attempting to connect to a MAN who is not programmed to meet to your expectations or is simply not suitable for a permanent hookup. Again, not every MAN is husband material.

Some partner models are made for recreational use while others are what I call "professional grade." How ironic that people study for every other role they fulfill except the most complex role of all — that of a married person. An honest assessment of the marriage workforce reveals that few are prepared to perform the often difficult tasks. The fact is, to make love work, you have to choose someone who is interested in more than game-playing.

Some may have spurts of ambition and attempt to maintain a love connection, but the relationship will be inconsistent at best. I often compare men who make big promises but can't back them up to "recreational use" models: they start off well, appearing to be capable of handling and providing a large capacity of love, but they are built for only limited loads of responsibility. The moment they reach full capacity, they bail.

The professional grade model, however, has been created to handle both the enormous love and endless obligations and responsibilities associated with an enduring connection. He has sturdy, built-in reserves for processing drama, trauma, and the unexpected. His hardware can handle fluctuations and knows how to stand by until energy has returned to full capacity in the relationship.

In short, this part doesn't quit on You when the going gets rough. As You consider the qualities of your MAN, take time to consider whether You could live with him forever as he is—with no changes made. You will then know if he is recreational or professional grade.

Ask yourself these questions: Are You merely entertained by him and find his attention enjoyable as long as You don't have to trust him with the major decisions of your life? Can You live with this MAN, who is limited in how much he can love or support You? Or are You able to trust this MAN and know that You can follow and submit to him because he has proven his willingness to go the extra mile? Here's the truth: You already know, deep down in your inner workings, whether this MAN is good to and for You. But if you're desperate to form a permanent link, You may make a bad choice.

The Difference between Love and Lust
Now is the time to make sure that what you're feeling is the real love current and not just lust based on good physical chemistry. You may experience powerful feelings that are not necessarily love. They may be the delight of mutual attraction and/or being "deeply in like." Neither of these will last past the first major conflict in your union.

Remember good old Amnon, King David's son? He was deeply "in love" with his half sister Tamar to the point of illness. Oh, he just had to have her, so he raped her. The story then goes on to say that he hated her more than he once "loved" her. Tamar remained a broken recluse for the rest of her life and her brother eventually killed Amnon in revenge (see 2 Sam. 13).

Why am I telling You this story? To remind You not to assume that your feelings are based on the desire to love and give yourself to someone. It's just possible that your feelings are based on sensual desire, which may short out your ability to evaluate your potential union with the MAN. Know for certain—perhaps seek premarital counseling to make sure you're both operating on a current of love. For long-term relationships, lust doesn't work. Only love does.

The Last Step before Merging

Once you've gathered all your data, heeded any warning signals, and settled that this MAN is the only MAN for YOU, one step remains. In order to ensure the perfect love connection, YOU must shatter the fear virus. Fear will act as a negative firewall and will hinder even the most avid lover from completing a love connection.

This virus is sometimes invisible, though the effect it has on the relationship is highly visible. Some partners don't realize it's present until the day of the wedding. They can't complete the process because of cold feet.

That's the mild side of it. I know you're thinking of the romantic comedy *Runaway Bride*, starring Julia Roberts. But remember also the recent real-life drama when a woman, overwhelmed by the idea of marriage, actually staged her own kidnapping!

It's true: YOU and the MAN may seem to be sharing the same current, but it's possible that at the last minute, one of you will bolt. Or you may never make it to the initial engagement. YOU can disable fear in a couple of ways.

First, maintain connection with the GOD part, which is able to shield your commitment from destruction and empower YOU to focus intently on developing your love for the other person.

Share your fears freely with GOD and with your potential spouse—have the courage to put everything on the table. If between the MAN's encouragement and GOD's empowerment, YOU can't get past your fear, *don't plug in*. Only when your desire for a lifelong partnership with the MAN is stronger than your fear will love override fear and cancel it.

Second, keep in mind that any two people attempting to come together will be vulnerable to pain and trauma. No matter how well

You and the MAN make love work, life will still happen. The bottom line is that becoming one requires both partners to see that the reward of making love work far outweighs any fear of pain. No risk, no glorious gain.

Once You have completed all the steps we've described so far, you're ready: prepare to turn on!

INSIDER'S LOVE TIP
Be sure to thoroughly inspect your love machine before merging. Make sure that flying sparks aren't the only energy powering your relationship. Love is the real "juice" that will allow you to go the distance.

Turning On

The power of agreement is one of the most powerful forces in the universe. Remember the Tower of Babel? "The LORD said, 'If as one people speaking the same language they have begun to do this, then nothing they plan to do will be impossible for them'" (Gen. 11:6 NIV).

As two people agree to commit, connect, plug into and empower each other, love begins to do its best work in both You and the MAN. What a turn-on! The power to remain connected regardless of external or internal pressure in the form of temptations, failings, hard times, financial fallout, poor health, and all the other things that can assault both parts can only be achieved by being committed to the commitment you will make.

Authentic parts function according to their design and wiring regardless of surrounding conditions. They remain true to their function. The Manufacturer created You and the MAN for love. Don't hold back—celebrate your need for each other and expect that it will change you.

Finally: True Love!

It's time to make a commitment to your partner: to either marry or agree to see each other exclusively. If the former, You announce before GOD and family and other witnesses that You are willing to secure your link, exchange power for power, and forsake all other connections. For those who are dating seriously, you might be moving toward engagement unless obstacles appear.

It can be frightening and exhilarating all at the same time! In order to commit, both parts must expose their most vulnerable inner workings. This is the scariest part of making a connection, yet it is the most necessary. The areas of need You and the Man fulfill for each other will solidify your connection.

Both people must be willing to be naked and unashamed, withholding nothing, for your love connection to be effectual. It is in the transparent disclosure of both of you that you forge a solid bond and release your power to supply what the other part needs. This is the foundation of the two becoming one (see Eph. 5:31). This is what separates platonic friendship from courtship. Learning to be open with each other lays the foundation for deep intimacy when you decide to take your relationship to the next level. The things you share, the things reserved for only the two of you to know, become the element that fuses you together. Together with the God part, you form a cord that cannot easily be broken except by human choice (see Eccl. 4:12).

Sexual Intimacy

The final level of "knowing" is sexual intimacy. This should not be attempted until You have completed all other steps of assembly and *after* You have forged a permanent connection. Note: that would mean You are married.

A fusion is made in heaven that lights up the room and is apparent to all observers: a love connection has truly been ignited. The power you exchange in your committed relationship makes both of you even more powerful. Perhaps this is where the term "power couple" originated! It is this power surge that becomes contagious to everyone around you.

The Manufacturer designed this type of "knowing" to be a binding element. If initiated prematurely, sexual intimacy creates great confusion. Perhaps this is why the world calls it "making love," although we know it is impossible to manufacture love. Sex is one of the most powerful functions of the love machine and must be handled with great care as it is the closest thing to worship you will experience on earth. One of the words for worship in Greek is *proskuneo*, which means to kiss.

When Adam "knew" Eve, it was in the most intimate sense: the actual sexual act. As we humble and bare our souls before our Creator, worshiping or "kissing" Him, we make the ultimate connection that can only be imitated here on earth. For this reason, I believe that we spend a lifetime searching for a "soul mate" when what we truly crave is an eternal kiss that no temporal MAN can provide.

Only the Manufacturer can sustain an eternal link between us and Himself. The pleasure we experience in our earthly connection is simply a foretaste of the pleasure we will experience when we finally become one with Him throughout eternity. We will need glorified bodies after life on earth because the human body could not contain such an intense surge of pleasure indefinitely.

In both worship and sexual intimacy, YOU give all YOU are and all YOU have to the one YOU love. Neither act should be performed with temporary attachments, or even with a soon-to-be permanent attachment, as people do get left standing at the altar. Remember that no one in your life deserves this form of intimacy until he is permanently committed to protecting, providing, and maintaining YOU. (We will go into further detail about this in the Accessories section of this guide.)

Remember both YOU and the MAN must be prepared to receive each other. This is why initializing is so important. Courtship reveals things that casual or platonic friendship never will. In courtship, shifts in expectations on both of your parts reveal how intentional both of you will be in serving and loving each other. This information is crucial to defining who you both are and establishing whether you are compatible enough to form the permanent link of marriage.

As Time Goes By

Every person has the power to turn love on or off. Love is not controlled by emotion. Contrary to popular thought, love is driven by the decisions of the people involved. Therefore, You must decide to love. The MAN must decide to love You back. The love current is ruled by the strength of your commitment to your partner, not by what he does to stimulate it. While love *can* grow or diminish based upon what each partner does, its consistency should remain grounded in your decision to love.

Now you've taken a big step. Hopefully, you've already determined that your love is going to go the distance—bailing is not an option. When You *have* to make it work, You find a way to do so. If You give yourself other options—hooking up with a more compatible part, disconnecting from the GOD or MAN parts—they serve as excuses not to go the extra mile required to get your love back on track. This is something You prepare yourself for if You are in the dating phase—rose-colored glasses are out; reality is very in vogue if you're truly interested in being equipped to do the work it takes to make love last.

You know better (I hope). You know that making the decision to work at love is well worth the reward that will come from your efforts. (If You don't know this, *don't turn on the switch!* You'll only blow a fuse and do potentially permanent damage to the one You promised to love.)

If, however, your connection remains intact, You will begin to glow. After You plug in, the amazing love You share and all the possibilities it affords You to grow will challenge others to examine their own love connections. The power that love generates when it is properly connected should always have effects that extend beyond the couple involved. When positioned properly, your love should spark affection, healing, strength, joy, and peace in those who encounter You.

> **INSIDER'S LOVE TIP**
> Love is more powerful than death, yet it is more delicate than the finest china. Handle it and all extensions with care.

Congratulations! You've followed the Manufacturer's Manual guidance and learned how to make love work. You're ready to experience the truth that love brings light to the darkest of places internally as well as externally. Now that You have formed a connection, get ready to experience another great power surge!

3

Maintenance:
Preventive

Love is . . .
Patient and kind . . .
Patience
Kindness

Love is . . .
Not jealous or boastful or proud . . .
Trust
Humility

Love . . .
Does not demand its own way . . .
Sacrifice

Love . . .
Is not irritable,
Grace
And it keeps no record of when it has been
wronged.
Forgiveness

Love . . .
Is never glad about injustice
But rejoices whenever the truth wins out.
Integrity

Love
Never gives up,
Perseverance
Never loses faith,
Faith
And endures through every circumstance . . .
Faithfulness.

Congratulations! If you've just experienced your first installment of power from your love connection, You are still in the euphoria stage. According to research, this can last up to a year before the chemicals released with the first surge of love begin to wane. Then—and every union of parts experiences this—You need to supplement your love to experience continued bliss in order to maintain a healthy love flow to both parts.

You know You want to keep this feeling alive. Despite this, I find most people are not ready for the work required to keep love generating at its highest capacity. Therefore you find lots of couples walking around looking like deer caught in headlights or mumbling to themselves, "This was not what I expected!"

Be forewarned: if You want to move forward in your relationship—or even keep it at the level you've experienced so far—work will be involved. Whether You are in the committed courtship phase or a newlywed, this section applies to You. You should begin to utilize these principles during the courtship phase and continue to use them even more after You say your vows. This means You will need to heed serious maintenance guidelines to get the best results from your love relationship.

You've got to work love to make it work for You. Love is not generated or transferred by osmosis or wishes. It is generated when two partners act together to build unity. This unity preserves, nurtures, and grows the incredible gift called love.

Keep in mind that as You apply the steps needed to maintain this complex engine, doing it once will never be enough. In other words, maintaining love will require the effort You exerted to get the MAN in the first place.

Depending on what you as a couple face, a rebooting of your love engines may be necessary from time to time. When it comes to love, work is progressive and unending. I can vouch for the successful couples I know: it's taken a lot of work to get their love up and running, to synchronize their programs, and to generate mutually satisfying output.

There are two levels of maintenance: preventive and long-term. If You practice both, You will find that your love connection is seldom or never interrupted. If You skip any of the maintenance steps, You will experience unnecessary problems.

The maintenance program I recommend comes straight from the Manufacturer's Manual, under the section labeled 1 Corinthians 13. At the time, the apostle Paul, one of God's top technical advisors, wrote this particular chapter, he was addressing a bunch of gifted people who thought they should be loved just because of their gifted natures. But they had become a bit obnoxious and not so lovable.

The lesson here is You can be as beautiful, intelligent, wealthy, and witty as all get-out, but if You are not a loving individual You will miss the greatest part of love: lavishing it on someone else and receiving the residual reward of his enthusiastically returning your attention and affection. Remember: if You are sooo busy loving yourself, there will be no room or need for others to love You. Trust me: love does not work at its best when left to generate on its own.

Patience

To solidify the love connection between You and the Man, you'll both need to develop patience. The patience program serves as a sort of buffer between parts, smoothing over rough spots in the initial union. Now that you've committed to a serious relationship, as in courtship or marriage, You will find that you'll need to make numerous adjustments.

Once the initial rush of adrenaline and endorphins subsides, the rose-colored hue of the relationship fades. Women are startled to find that men leave toilet seats up and their socks in inconvenient places, not to mention the condition of the shower. New husbands find out that the women who once thought everything they did was attractive now find those same actions irritating. If you've been in the courtship phase for a while, his jokes might not be as funny as they once were, or You may discover a quirky habit, but don't let these things scare You. You probably have something that is freaking him out, too! Say to yourself, "This is just a test!" Because truly it is.

A battle of personalities and wills ensues, with men and women choosing their corners—their particular ways of doing things—and stubbornly sticking to them. Warning: this approach will not strengthen your love connection but will start a subtle corrosion that could lead to cracks and chinks in your alignment.

Your success as a couple—the deciding factor for whether you will make love work—will depend on how pliable and flexible both parts are. Making the necessary adjustments to accommodate each other can be difficult, but it's always doable if both partners are willing.

Patience: Its Power to Transform

I mentioned earlier that patience is the tool that uncovers deceit. It is also a tool with great transforming powers. If YOU practice patience while downloading the various programs YOU want to operate during your relationship, these programs will be installed successfully and work for years to come. If, however, YOU choose to rush the installation process, YOU could experience locking, stalling, or, heaven forbid, a complete crash of the love unit. Do not overload your MAN's circuits by trying to force the MAN to be the part YOU want him to be overnight. It simply won't work and will cause a major breakdown in your love flow.

Change is scary for both parts, since relationships tend to demand more change than anyone ever expects! During the initial attraction period, both parts often look perfect to each other. But circumstances may reveal that both parts need significant improvement. The truth of the matter is, neither of you is perfect and YOU need to be willing to make whatever changes are necessary. Here is where patience comes in and smoothes the conflict.

Patience Waits

Patience observes and waits. It waits for the MAN to desire change for himself. Patience can be the salvation of your relationship. We see this demonstrated to perfection by the GOD part. GOD waits for us to choose to connect to Him without being pushy or forward. GOD is not willing that anyone perish, yet He waits for each person to choose connection to Him. It is His patience that makes Him so appealing. He graciously allows us to make our own choices, and we should do the same with our partners.

Patience Empowers

> Patience is empowering because it leaves room for your partner to make the right choice on his own.

This is something You need to learn before You are permanently linked to your mate; it will make the transition from singleness to married life ultimately a lot smoother. The woman who patiently picks up those socks and puts them away without saying anything saves herself a lot of drama. Her partner will be moved to pick up his own socks sooner or later because he will be convicted by how gracious You are, in spite of his habit.

True, some men may never pick up their socks (or complete equally trivial tasks the way You want them to). What's a woman to do in a case like that? You should not allow something as mundane as socks to rule your character and disposition. It's really about accepting people for who they are and allowing them the room to grow and transform without coercing them to do things against their will. Remember, even God allows everyone the awesome privilege of free will! In the movie *The Breakup*, Jennifer Aniston's character was upset with Vince Vaughn's character because he agreed begrudgingly to help her with the dishes. Her point of contention was that she didn't just want him to help with the dishes—she wanted him to *want* to help. The disaster that followed led to an even bigger blowup, which cost them both more than they wanted to pay by the time the relationship was over. The bad feelings created from a conflict about socks are just not worth the toll they take on the relationship. To pick up the socks and move on is not only an act of service but also an act of grace for your partner that will eventually influence the really important matters in a relationship (if both parts really want the connection to stay strong).

The Manufacturer's Manual tells us, "The end of a matter is better than its beginning, and patience is better than pride" (Eccl. 7:8 NIV).

I'm talking about winning a man over not by your words but by your behavior! This is a tool that is subtle but powerful and very worth mastering if You want to get anywhere with your Man.

I realized one day that when my dog does something she is not supposed to, I don't get that excited. I gently correct her and move on. This realization gave me pause: why was I able to be so patient with her? I knew it wasn't only because she's awfully cute. I'm patient with her because I know my dog is imperfect. She is, after all, just a dog. I don't harbor unrealistic expectations, so her imperfections don't irritate me. You see where I'm going with this?

Impatience often comes from overblown expectations. When it comes to love connections, You don't necessarily need to lower your standards; You just need to make room for people messing up until they know better and choose to do better. Remember that your partner has been doing things one way for a very long time, so it will take time to form a new habit.

Again, though, sometimes he will never choose to do better. Depending on the seriousness of his bad habit—only You can determine whether his habit is irritating, self-destructive, or dangerous—you'll either have to develop more patience, get outside help, or disconnect until you can be realigned.

Everyone responds more readily to patience and consideration than criticism. True patience is able to overlook small offenses or irritations. It stabilizes both partners until they are able to operate on a mutual wavelength. Let's face it: God waits whole lifetimes for us to get properly connected to Him and learn to do things in a way that pleases Him. Yet as mere mortals, we tend to demand more from each other than God does!

Patience's Best Example

I think I love Jesus most for His patience with folks, especially with that motley crew, His disciples. He had lived with them for three years, but they still reacted impetuously, asked stupid questions, and failed to understand all He told them about Himself. But Jesus never gave up on them!

I suppose He just sighed and perhaps counted to ten. Then He would ask, "How long have you been with me?" He understood their frailty, their fears, their pasts, and the experiences that colored their responses, and He gave the disciples time to grow in love and understanding.

He gave them the power to choose His way of life for themselves. The result? The world has never been the same.

How to Use Patience Properly

In order to use patience effectively, you need to follow a few guidelines.

1. Think before You Speak or Act

You've heard this a hundred times, but that's just because it's good advice. Speaking or acting first and thinking later never smoothes a conflict. Rash reactions and knee-jerk responses create unnecessary static in the relationship that jams communication, hinders resolution, and actually magnifies the problem beyond its true proportions.

2. Look at the Big Picture and Pick Your Battles

Go ahead and admit it: every little mistake is not that crucial. But every little criticism and negative conversation can add up to a major war—one You may lose due to lack of patience. Confrontation at every turn and an endless list of demands can actually repel your partner rather than get him to line up with your desires (see Prov. 21:19).

Decide what your long-term goal is with this MAN. Is making an issue into a major conflict conducive to getting what You ultimately want? Don't get me wrong. Having patience does not mean that You never say anything. It is the *way* You say things, and when, that counts. Patience speaks calmly and quietly and waits until the heat of the moment has passed so that the truth can be spoken in love (see Prov. 15:1).

3. Don't Make Him Defensive

Patience does not condemn your partner or make him feel defensive. If You are patient, You will respectfully state what You need from your partner to accomplish a greater sense of harmony (see Rom. 12:18). Patience always seeks peace and reconciliation.

Peace and reconciliation, you see, are patience's main functions. You can't fight with someone and try to reach a peaceful end at the same time. Slowly and deliberately, patience helps You accept the imperfection of your partner while leaving room for improvement without pressure.

Patience overlooks offenses while gently correcting and encouraging. In this way, You keep your connection with the Man free from resentment and other feelings that could sabotage the way your love works. Subtle persuasion ignites good feelings in both parts. Why? Because through patience, each person feels empowered to do the right thing in the interest of the other partner, thus increasing the love flow. And free-flowing love will always work!

INSIDER'S LOVE TIP
Patience is best exercised when operated free from the output of other extensions whose opinions may be based on their own personal interests. In other words, what happens at your house should stay at your house. Kinda like Las Vegas.

Kindness

K indness, gentleness, goodness: all of these components work together to create a sustained electrical charge between You and the Man. Just as "a gentle answer turns away wrath" (Prov. 15:1 NIV), kindness creates favor for the giver. Favor, in turn, opens the floodgates for love to operate at optimum capacity.

The kindness and patience programs feed off of each other, creating an atmosphere conducive to love's operating at its best. Because kindness generates such good feelings, there is no such thing as too much of it. It is something that everyone appreciates and wants. Kindness nurtures intimacy.

And it's clear from the Manufacturer's Manual that He wants us to practice it: "As God's chosen people, holy and dearly loved, clothe yourselves with compassion, kindness, humility, gentleness and patience" (Col. 3:12 NIV).

How to Practice Kindness

Be Sensitive
Sensitivity is key if You want to practice kindness effectively. To be sensitive, You must be totally engaged with your partner's life and mind. This engagement requires You to be present—really hear and see his unspoken moods and needs. You "listen between the lines" because You are locked on him, not only physically but spiritually and emotionally as well.

If YOU are sensitive, YOU use everything in your power to tune in to your partner. YOU are connected. This is the power of being one. The invisible current that flows between you makes you more sensitive to each other's needs and feelings. YOU sense when the current changes and his mood shifts. YOU begin to anticipate his needs before he tells YOU about them, and YOU respond before being asked.

Of course, being sensitive is easier said than done! Life is full of distractions—including our own needs, moods, and feelings. Being present to your partner requires some mastery of your MIND and HEART. The more YOU have on your plate, the more effort it will take to tune in, but tune in YOU must for the sake of the relationship.

We see in the Manufacturer's Manual that Jesus pulled this off nicely by asking tons of questions or by answering them in an open-ended way that left room for the people He was talking with to reveal more than they otherwise might have. By the end of His discussions with people, they had disclosed themselves fully to Him—and to themselves!

In His conversation with a young man who wanted eternal life, Jesus made him an offer he refused: to give up all he had to the poor and follow the Son of God (Matt. 19:16–22). Jesus' requirement, and the young man's refusal, revealed the young man's heart to both of them. The man went away sorry because he did not want to make the sacrifice Jesus suggested. His possessions meant more to him than he realized. In John 5:1–7, Jesus asked a man who was paralyzed if he wanted to be well. A good question, since some people enjoy their paralysis. Jesus got to the heart of the matter and the man was cured. Later, Jesus asked Peter time and time again what he loved most, provoking Peter to examine his priorities (John 21:15–17). When YOU are sensitive and caring, your words carry real weight.

Stay Strong with the GOD Part

Remaining plugged into the GOD part will empower YOU to practice greater levels of kindness. Yes, there it is again: the GOD part as your most powerful source of love. The more consistent your connection to God, the better your ability to output large amounts of kindness, patience, and love. When running on your own power, You will be hard-pressed to keep a continual flow.

The God part will also alert You to things You might miss in your interaction with the Man. God enhances your spiritual sensitivity as You take the time to commune with Him first thing in the morning and throughout the day. In the quiet times when your spirit is open to His instruction, You will be amazed at the insight He will give You on your partner—as well as on the issues of your own life.

When You are connected first to God, You will have access to all the resources You need to practice kindness, which will help keep your love connection strong. Remember that You can run on reserve power for only a limited time, so purpose to reboot regularly in order to enhance your spiritual and emotional acuity.

The Way Kindness and Patience Interact

Kindness empowers patience to operate at full capacity because kindness empowers You to remain true to who God created You to be—one who displays His character in all facets.

> In some instances, kindness will be mistaken for weakness—but You need STRENGTH to be kind.

Kindness requires strength, especially if the Man is functioning in an erratic manner. A fool can bring out the fool in You if You have not mastered kindness. If You can keep your cool, maintain your composure, You will find that kindness or goodness always overcomes evil (Rom. 12:21). Prayer is a mandatory program that must be installed and utilized regularly in order for your system to function properly and not lock up when pushed to resist bad behavior or purposeful sabotage of your love connection.

If you're having trouble practicing kindness, check your heart. Remember, the server can hinder or empower the output of kindness. Serving is a lost art in today's culture, but it is a hidden treasure that hosts a great degree of power. The greater your ability to yield yourself in service, the greater your capacity to give and receive kindness and love.

The Powers of Good Service

Have you ever been served at a restaurant by a waiter who acted as if he were doing you a favor, even though you were paying for the service? When I encounter that attitude, I'm always tempted to leave a note saying, "My tip for today is this: when you give better service, you'll get a bigger tip."

On the other hand, I've eaten at places where the food wasn't that great but the service was so wonderful that I was very generous with my tip. Good service sometimes overshadows bad food.

It's been said that we often treat family like strangers and strangers like family: we're much nicer to those we don't have to live with. Though familiarity can breed contempt, it shouldn't. The sin of complacency is the silent killer of a servant's heart and in turn, kindness. If You are complacent, You think or say to your spouse, "Get it yourself. Must I do everything for You? By the way, what have You done for me lately?"

Because God does not promise You a tomorrow, it should always be a privilege to serve the one You love (see Gal. 5:13). The minute your mind-set changes to how your partner is serving You, the power of your exchange wanes, and the chemistry between you will diminish. Kindnesses are another form of kisses but on a deeper level—one that touches the Soul of the Man and woos him. Yes, kindness has the "woo" factor!

Everyone is drawn to kindness. We want to spend more and more time in the presence of those who do kind things that make us feel special and wanted. Kindness is like a magnet that attracts the Man to You and ignites electricity between you even when you're apart.

The good memories of your loving service will linger in the man's MIND. They offer silent reminders of your presence that stir feelings of pleasure within the MAN. Kindness will make the MAN smile in the middle of the day for no reason—or even inspire him to bring home a pleasant surprise or call in the middle of the day just to say, "I love You."

INSIDER'S LOVE TIP
Kindness is the special ingredient that leaves imprints on the SOUL of a MAN. It works its own brand of magic with long-lasting effects.

The bottom line is that kindness begets kindness. So practice this form of preventive maintenance: do unto others as You would have them do unto You. Ultimately, that makes love work for everyone!

Trust

Your union is both intensely strong and delicate. In order for it to function well, special programming is essential. I've mentioned some of them already, but here is an especially potent one: trust. Without it, the union of You and the MAN—in committed courtship or in matrimony—begins to weaken and actually break into pieces. As time goes by, you'll find it increasingly hard to function at all. Your love connection may suffer a permanent severance.

To secure a love connection that lasts, you simply must build trust. Though it takes a while to build, it can be destroyed in a moment. Yes, trust can be shaken or ruptured by a word or act. And no trust means no love connection, plain and simple.

How to Build Trust

Do What You Say You'll Do

How is trust built? Through integrity. Someone once said that on a job, a person should promise little and do much more. The same could be said of love. God models this perfectly: He delivers everything He promises, from the son that elderly Sarah dared not hope for to a long-awaited Messiah for the nation of Israel.

God cannot lie—He would be acting against His own nature. Anyone who claims to know God must also line up with and operate in truth. To make love work, couples must be attuned to each other's patterns and preferred routines. Here comfort levels are set and established in the love unit. Fluctuating love levels indicate that something is wrong, and you need to find out what.

When both partners get used to each other's modes of behavior, they develop trust on an unspoken level. They need to be able to rely on each other.

> A union functions better if partners follow through for each other in a trustworthy manner.

Irregularities cause trauma to our HEARTS that can cripple the love flow or, at best, cause complications. Men especially are known to be set in their ways—stuck in one program. They prefer routines to sudden changes. Don't rock his world by flipping the script drastically without warning. It will set him totally off-kilter, and a man who feels out of control can totally implode or shut down on YOU—this is not good for YOU or the relationship. If the MAN's change of behavior puts your HEART on alert, with warning lights flashing and buzzers beeping wildly, YOU may put all your love systems on hold indefinitely until YOU are able to relax again, and vice versa.

Love can stop working as a response to something as seemingly mundane as a broken promise from your partner to call YOU at a certain time. This forgetfulness is common among men simply because they cannot multitask and tend to be in-the-moment types. If they're distracted, they can drop the ball. It's important to realize that YOU don't need to panic about a missed phone call unless it becomes a repeated malfunction.

If he repeatedly makes promises to call but fails to do so, calmly remind him that integrity is important to YOU, and repeats of this insensitive behavior will cause YOU to question the security of the connection between you. Simply stating your need should be enough to put him on alert if YOU are truly important to him.

If his repeated malfunctions increase, take heed: YOU may be connected to a broken part! In this case, love will struggle to function before failing to work any longer. Trust must work without fluctuating in order to secure love (see Ps. 36:7).

In a world of uncertainty, everyone is in search of security. No one wants to invest in a mechanism or program that will crash, lose important data, or rupture a hard drive. You need to be able to depend on your partner to maintain all things vital to the love connection without erasing pertinent information, damaging delicate parts, or severing crucial links. A malfunction of the love unit can leave both components alone and with no power.

Should inconsistencies occur within the patterns your partner has set, he needs to save You from unnecessary trauma or dangerous speculation by informing You of his circumstances. You may need to ask for this reassurance. Of course, this works both ways. If You promise more than You can deliver and repeatedly fail, your partner has every right to question your integrity.

The bottom line is that both parts need to be secure in the knowledge that their relationship is solid. You and the MAN need to know you can always count on each other. You want to know that your partner has your best interest at heart and vice versa.

If the trust program is not installed, insecurity may put You or the MAN in search mode. Both of you will continue to search until you find other parts to whom you can attach—people you can trust. This is not what the Manufacturer designed you for.

If you've installed trust well, when such inconsistencies occur you will wait (or ask, if You need to) for an explanation and expect the best of your partner.

Communicate

Communication is key to trust. It keeps partners clear on where they stand with each other.

I dated a rock star for a short season. You can imagine that nothing breeds insecurity like dating someone wanted by hundreds, thousands, or millions of other women! But he and I had already discussed how he felt about other women's excessive attention and how he felt about me, and he did everything to assure me that though women were literally throwing their bodies at him when we were out in public together, he was leaving with me. I felt safe and empowered to find the humor in what could have been unnerving circumstances and to trust him completely. Our communication even freed me to smile and be gracious with those women. I knew I had his heart, which prevented a lot of conflict and fear for me. (Our relationship later dissolved for completely different reasons.)

In love, it is generally unsafe to make assumptions. Assumptions are usually based on feelings, not facts, and our past hurts and painful relationships may affect our vision. Heartbreak can create negative illusions that overshadow reality.

The more the two of you communicate, the greater the level of trust you will establish. Through the consistency of exchange, you will learn each other's MINDS, which will enable you to anticipate each other's actions more readily.

As You learn what triggers reactions or behaviors in each other, you will know what buttons not to push to keep each other from shutting down or blowing a fuse.

Communication is key in building trust because it creates intimacy. Intimacy, both physical and emotional, binds two people together.

One of the things that makes the love connection thrive is your feeling safe with each other. Communication helps you maintain this feeling. Reliability is a connector in your relationship. Both parts—You and the MAN—must be able to celebrate the life that trust and integrity bring to your connection.

The Way Integrity Works

Integrity must do more than keep a person from casual lies or even adultery. Integrity is essential in your day-to-day exchange. For integrity to operate efficiently, a few things must occur.

1. Share the Truth in Love

You must be willing to risk your partner's displeasure by sharing truth with him that will make him a better person for You as well as himself.

2. Absorb the Truth in Love

You must be willing to acknowledge the truth when your partner confronts You with words or behaviors that You might not want to face. Integrity means that You own your stuff even when it is difficult because it is the truth that will set you free—free to love and free to go deeper in your relationship with your partner. Why? Because You will be casting off things that hinder love from flowing at its greatest strength.

3. Use Truth to Deepen Your Relationship

Love gives You the freedom to share from the heart all thoughts and even desires. Because both of you love truth, you recognize that when one of you expresses an emotion or thought, it is an invitation to deepen the connection by choosing the right response. Sometimes the truth hurts, but it must be recognized in order for the relationship to progress.

> Truth demands growth, and when both parts recognize truth in a revelation, they can celebrate because they know they have the chance to take love to another level.

Without truth, there can be no growth. Without truth, there can be no bond between the parts. Truth helps your partner anticipate your needs and gives him open access to your heart.

4. Use Integrity to Build Trust

Truth breeds trust. Dishonesty sets both parts off-kilter and corrodes the comfort factor between you.

I previously mentioned the little inconsistencies that threaten a relationship. One "little white lie" has hurt many a relationship because it puts the deceived person on guard. *If YOU lied about this, what else will YOU lie about? Now YOU cannot be trusted.* A lie is not only what is spoken; sometimes it can be what is unspoken and left to assumption. The wall a part puts up is hard to remove or penetrate. Here begins the disintegration of the bond in the relationship because honesty stops flowing readily. And when parts withhold, they create a strain on the connection.

If, however, both parts practice integrity, they will grow closer and allow no walls to form in their relationship. *"He whose walk is blameless and who does what is righteous, who speaks the truth from his heart . . . who keeps his oath even when it hurts . . . He who does these things will never be shaken"* (Ps. 15:2, 4–5 NIV, emphasis mine).

It's Personal

When all is said and done, you and your partner's ability to trust will be powered by your personal levels of trustworthiness. Those who are faithful themselves will expect faithfulness from their partners. Those who are untrustworthy will never be able to trust their partners. Their own instability will ignite fear, which will completely cancel out trust.

We all tend to see people through the lens of our own behavior: how we ourselves operate. Perfect love has to kick in for us to change how we view people. The more we love, the more we trust simply because love always seeks and believes the best of the other person (see 1 Cor. 13:7).

Simply put, trust makes love work.

INSIDER'S LOVE TIP
Trust is beautiful and should be kept on constant display.

Humility

The deadliest virus known to kill love in record time is pride. Therefore, one must install a humility program at the onset of the love connection. Pride is the killer of honest communication and intimacy, patience, trust, and kindness. It will jam love circuits for indefinite amounts of time.

The moment one part becomes infected with this virus, the relationship is in danger. Self-importance will remove the need for the other part. Pride deceives a part into believing it can generate enough power to sustain itself on its own. It sets parts up for isolation and loneliness. It sabotages relationships by triggering parts to surround themselves with a shell that actually repels any further connection.

The Problem with Pride Started a Long Time Ago

I think of Ezekial 28:12–19 and Isaiah 14:12–16 of the Manufacturer's Manual, which some theologians believe allude to one of the most glorious angels, Lucifer. The Scriptures can be understood to say that he was the most beautiful of all God's creations and was once considered a son of God, perhaps even a favorite—at least that's my personal speculation. Since the Hebrew for "Lucifer" can also mean "light-bearer," some have speculated that Lucifer's job was to collect praise and worship and deliver it to God. It seems that one day he decided that he deserved all that praise and worship. He thought he should be God!

Imagine Lucifer spreading his dangerous ideas among a third of the heavenly host, who agreed to join him in rebellion. That's when he got the shock of his life. Though God loved him with a perfect love, He could not and would not tolerate Lucifer's attitude in the heavenlies, and He promptly booted the angel out. Lucifer was cast down from heaven and doomed to be forever separated from God. It's not the end Lucifer (now called Satan) expected, I'm sure. He's still bitter about it and taking his revenge by attempting to wreak havoc in our lives (see 1 Pet. 5:8).

Pride is dangerous because it can build over time. It slowly seeps into your thoughts, building a case for its destructive attitude, convincing You that You are all that and a bag of chips. Its case for self-importance becomes inflated the longer You dwell on it. It begins to stir up discontent that makes You overly demanding because You feel justified in expecting more: more love . . . more respect . . . more attention . . . more of everything, including some stuff You may not even need.

Pride downloads additional viruses of entitlement and unrealistic expectations to the system that can put a strain on the love unit. A part infected with pride is never satisfied with the amount of love or attention it receives. Pride sucks You into believing that You are GOD's gift to the MAN. This is actually true, but it's true only when You are operating in the humility mode. The MAN is also a gift to You! If You miss this truth, You will believe that the MAN should do whatever it takes to keep the relationship alive while You contribute nothing to the function of your unit.

Don't believe the hype. Follow this simple rule of thumb:

> If You have to demand admiration, respect, or even love, You haven't done the work to earn it.

What You demand will be difficult to maintain, but what You inspire will remain.

Pride Lies

Pride is a deceptive virus because its host is usually insecure. The false bravado is merely a shell for protecting a vulnerable heart. Pride can be downright obnoxious, and those who practice it don't benefit. Arrogant people set themselves up for major rejection. After all, if you're so impressed with yourself, You don't really leave room for anyone else to be. Not only does pride make You a noncontributor to making love work, it mars the qualities in You that inspire your partner to want to make love work!

Pride is destructive to a union because it hinders both partners from being open: open to change, correction, and growth that make the relationship richer. In short, pride comes before the fall, and many usually watch the isolated and ungraceful tumble.

It is vulnerability that makes both people able to embrace each other. When love is functioning properly in both partners, they don't feel the need to exalt themselves or to magnify their personal importance. Their focus is on pleasing the other person. Love drives You to build up your partner—to make him feel more special, more important than yourself. This actually makes You feel good!

You see, it really takes great strength to operate in humility, meekness, and vulnerability. We see in the Manufacturer's Manual that humility draws God closer to us: "All of you, clothe yourselves with humility toward each other, because, 'God opposes the proud but gives grace to the humble'" (1 Pet. 5:5 NIV).

Humility Is All Good

Humility Is the Key to Gaining Importance

There is something about humility that is downright sexy and appealing. It draws love, respect, and honor to itself like a magnet. When someone is unimpressed with herself, even when she should be impressed, she becomes more attractive. To consider others as more important than yourself is the key to gaining importance. The way up is truly down.

In the end, cultivating the heart of a servant gets you served. If Jesus, who was the King of kings and Lord of lords, could wash the feet of a motley crew of men, cook them breakfast, and serve them, who are we to think we are above serving others? And why would we not want to serve the ones we love? When it's love, it won't feel like work to serve at all.

Let's face it: people have been willing to die for Jesus. Could it be because He makes them feel more loved and more valued than they ever felt before?

Humility Helps Us Love as We Want to Be Loved

In a world where we are all taught that we need to have healthy self-esteem, no one explains how to tell when You have too much. We can actually come to love ourselves so much we can't love others properly. The Manufacturer's Manual does encourage us to love ourselves, but we are to do so because loving ourselves enables us to love our neighbors or significant others (see Gal. 5:14).

In other words, You can know what it takes to make another person feel significant and cared for by using what You need yourself as a realistic barometer. The instruction to love yourself was never about staring at your belly button so closely that You don't even notice when you've walked over someone else. No, no, for love to work steadily and effectively, You must be willing to get over yourself and serve your partner. As we've seen, serving is one of the main functions of love.

Humility Enables You to Find Honor in Serving

Only those who embrace and exude humility are able to find honor in serving another person. Only they will experience true love and fulfillment because they are willing to pour themselves out completely for the sake of others.

Humility Begets Forgiveness

Humility also generates forgiveness. Should You do something that offends your partner, if You are humble You will correct and delete the error, confess, ask forgiveness, and willingly allow him to override any conflicting input from You for the sake of reconciliation.

Humble people pick their battles carefully. They value people over the principle of the matter. They choose remaining in the relationship over being right and seek peace above all things. They are not bent on proving their point. They allow others to rise or fall on their own, never pushing them over the edge to get the best of them. They give grace to other people, and therefore, they also receive it. They know that no one is perfect and actually rejoice in that fact.

Humility Empowers You in the Relationship

Humility makes You powerful in the relationship because You learn to give of yourself even when your partner is being unlovely. No one can take advantage of You when You embrace humility. No one will have the power to embarrass You, offend You, or hurt You because You will not harbor expectations that set You up for disappointment.

This does not mean You should not have expectations; it simply means that You are able to yield your right to them. It is our so-called rights that get us into trouble and complicate how love works. Especially when our partners have "rights" of their own!

The people who consider themselves of no importance become the power conduits in relationships. These people will step beneath the others and lift them up. They refuse to be selfish or operate out of empty conceit; rather, with humility of mind, they choose to regard their partners as more important than themselves. We get our most amazing picture of humility from the Manufacturer's Manual in Philippians 2:3–8.

Obviously, this picture of humility flies in the face of all self-esteem teaching, and I am certainly not talking about submitting to abuse. Yet the greatest secret to gaining power is yielding it by your own choice, which leaves nothing for anyone to take (see Matt. 5:38–42). After all, if You choose to give, how can someone feel as if they gained the upper hand over You? Talk about diffusing a swollen ego! Remember that Jesus said that no one took His life; He laid it down (see John 10:17–18). In the end, He gained everything!

Another thing: the woman who treats her husband like a king usually gets treated like a queen without having to ask (that is, if her husband embraces humility as well).

Humble people's willingness to admit when they are wrong opens the floodgates to healing and forgiveness. They understand that a relationship is not a relationship if only one is present after being wounded. They realize that six of the most costly words to say—"I'm sorry; will you forgive me?"—are more expensive when they are not said.

Two becoming one has everything to do with absorbing offense and each other's pain in the interest of loving to a greater capacity.

Humility Lets You Be Your Authentic Self

Perhaps the greatest benefit You will receive from operating in humility is that it releases You to be your authentic self, transparent, with all your strengths and weaknesses on full display. You become open to being loved just as You are—no need to demand it. And if You can't be real in love . . . well, it just won't work.

INSIDER'S LOVE TIP
Humility operates best when You choose, rather than are forced, to use it. There is a difference between humility and being humiliated—the choice is yours.

Sacrifice

Perhaps the hardest program of love to install is that of sacrifice. No one sees the merit of this program until after using it. This program must cancel out the preinstalled selfish program for love to work at maximum capacity.

One should not be embarrassed to find selfishness in place. Selfishness is automatically present at the onset of humanity. Babies are selfish: they instinctively call attention to their needs and can't control their demanding nature. Therefore, they cry until they get what they want. Never mind the fact that their parents might be exhausted and need sleep—if babies want comfort, food, a dry diaper, or attention, they want it now!

Suffice it to say that even though selfishness is preinstalled, it is still a sign of immaturity if it is never placed under control or removed. This is where sacrifice in a relationship comes in. Those who delay installing the sacrifice program in the center of their relationship find themselves engaged in struggles that threaten their love. The moment You insist that everything in the love relationship goes your way or the highway, love is heading down the wrong path—namely south.

The Nature of Sacrifice

Sacrifice Means Both Win
Love cannot function when a battle of the wills interrupts its operation, because it relies on the two becoming one in order to fuel it. Love needs *team coordinates* to function.

> Coordinating parts understand that in order to operate in a
> winning fashion, each partner must be willing to sacrifice func-
> tioning as a solo system for the greater good of the love unit.

Every team that wins a game has worked like a fine-tuned machine. So
must You and your partner. Even though You have the power to operate
and function effectively in an isolated window, You might need to minimize yourself on the screen to make room for the data that your partner's
program could add to the relationship. Being the star of your own program is great, but there is great power in being able to merge two separate
operating systems because they will function at a superior level.

YOU need to understand that when You are unwilling to sacrifice
for the greater good of the relationship You lose more in the end
than You initially had. For love to work as it should, sacrifice is absolutely necessary. Depending on the circumstances, either You or
the MAN will have to yield power for the betterment of the relationship—and that means you both win.

Sacrifice Is Ongoing
In essence, both You and the MAN will be required to "die" over and over
again throughout the relationship to preserve and strengthen it. Perhaps
this is why I sometimes accidentally call weddings "funerals"—not to
be morbid but to point out that when a couple says, "I do," it is the last
"I" that either of them owns. I can always tell how close a couple is by
whether the bride or groom continues to say "I" in conversation or "we."

Sacrifice Empowers YOU
Dying to self for the benefit of the one You love can be excruciating
because it requires You to put the good of your partner above yourself. This action is not the natural tendency of any human being,
and it requires decisive discipline. Still, the deeper your love for your
partner, the easier it will be to yield your power to him.

If love is not the motivation for giving and sacrifice, You will
feel it as duty rather than choice—choice that actually feeds and

empowers You, because it feels good to extend yourself for the one You love. You won't want to remain in a relationship that has You going through the motions without the right emotions.

The Obstacle to Sacrifice: Selfishness

Sacrifice is more difficult for some than others. You can become set in your ways, making even compromise difficult. The longer You remain single and autonomous, the more selfish You may tend to become.

Many things can contribute to selfishness. Let's look at a few of them.

Habits

Habits—the way You or he always does things—can be very hard to let go of. From deciding where things are placed in the house (if you're married) to giving up something You really wanted to accommodate the needs and/or wishes of your partner, the sudden necessity to share your space, time, resources, and self can be disconcerting. Sharing is something You have to get used to.

Many single women have joked that there is just not enough closet space for the men who would enter their worlds. I can second that emotion: it will be an adjustment to make room not just physically but also emotionally for someone else. Perhaps this is the reason so many have become commitment-phobic even though they say they long for love. The great question looms: *What do I have to give up in order to have love?*

Fear

Fear is a great enabler of selfishness. When You are afraid, You ferociously guard everything You hold dear because You don't trust anyone. Fear can stem from issues You had in past attachments as well as present self-involvement. By being crippled by past disappointments and heartbreak, You can subconsciously erect a personal firewall that is hard to break out of. No one can get in, but You can't get out.

It's very important for You to be honest with yourself, to own your fears and get rid of them. Check your motivations for doing what You do. Do You stay busy because You are involved with things You love or because being busy is a good distraction from the loneliness You fear? Do the things You do feed only You or do they contribute to the lives of others?

If You are not willing to experience even a little discomfort for the sake of someone else, take a look at that. What are You really protecting? I suggest it is more than your schedule.

Remember, love has the capacity to cancel fear, and You should use it to do so. Deciding to get rid of fear will require an act of your will over your feelings. You have more power than You know, so choose to superimpose love over your fears.

Boundaries

Selfishness is always justifiable to the person who is selfish. Some people are quick to remind others that You must set personal boundaries or people will take advantage of You. Though boundaries are good and necessary, unfortunately, many women put the wrong ones in place at the wrong times.

Good boundaries ensure the health of one person for the good of every other person she knows. Her boundaries let people know what her limits are so they can respect them, which nurtures healthy relationships for everyone concerned. But a person should not use boundaries to provide comfort for only herself, and if her comfort level exists at the expense of someone else's, she is selfish.

Some like to say they are not selfish, just self-*full*. They're one and the same. If a person is full of herself, she is indeed extremely selfish. It's all about her. The other person's feelings don't matter to her—even if it's someone she "loves." One person's selfishness feeds off her desire to do what is most convenient for her with total disregard of what her selfishness might cost the relationship.

A MAN once came into my life who was ready to scoop me up and marry me on the spot. But he had five children, had plenty of baby-mama drama, and was broke from paying for three households before he even got to his own personal maintenance. He declared, "I deserve to have someone like you after all that I've been through. My kids deserve to have someone like you."

I thought, *Do I deserve this?* After all, I had been minding my own business and enjoying a pretty uncomplicated life. I had to examine my heart to make sure I wasn't simply being selfish. He was a fantastic man in many ways, but I just wasn't sure I wanted all that came with him to the party. Was I stuck in my own selfish ways and running from the love I thought I wanted, or was I preparing to complicate my life unnecessarily?

I finally relinquished the relationship after several friends tackled me, pinned me to the ground, and shook sense into me. The consensus was: "This is not a good situation. See it for the destructive distraction that it is!"

I have to admit I felt relieved. Having a healthy sense of what is good for You and what You deserve cannot be confused with selfishness. The difference is that the healthy person looks at the big picture to decide if the situation would be destructive or constructive for *all* involved. Selfishness, on the other hand, is simple—only one person matters in the equation.

Entitlement

Another selfish attitude is "You owe it to yourself." Selfishness is deceptive, because it justifies itself with feelings of entitlement. It convinces You that you've already "sacrificed" enough for others when the truth is You will never sacrifice "enough." Love is an endless giving of yourself to the one You love. It is in the giving and sacrifice that You illuminate something even more awesome—what You get in return.

What about what You owe to your partner—or others in your circle? You owe it to the world to make a contribution. None of us should be guilty of taking up space or sucking up oxygen without giving something back. Selfishness leads to a lonely existence.

Eventually people figure out that You love yourself more than You love them and leave You to yourself. This desertion is usually a huge surprise to the selfish person because naturally, she doesn't think she is selfish at all!

Ordinary lovers become fantastic lovers when they learn that ultimate satisfaction comes from putting the pleasure of the beloved before their own. It is when You empty yourself that You make room for more pleasure and fulfillment than You ever imagined. If both people treat each other as the most important part of the relationship, both will get more than they anticipated.

The Surprise of Sacrifice

Sacrifice does not rob You of anything. In fact, in an equation that makes sense only with God in it, You gain the most by giving all that You have and all that You are to the one you love.

Because of His love, Christ sacrificed His life in order to save a dying world from sin. The more You are willing to sacrifice for your partner, the more love You generate in the relationship. Sacrifice is binding. We love Christ not only because He first loved us but also because He proved His love by giving His life to preserve ours. This is the ultimate gift of sacrifice: "Greater love has no one than this, that he lay down his life for his friends" (John 15:13 NIV).

In the midst of sacrifice, salvation will take place for both partners. As each person in the relationship dies to an element of him- or herself, new life will be generated. The two parts—You and the Man—will begin to increase in power, performance, and output.

The increase in positive output is the most evident sign that love is running—working—at maximum capacity!

INSIDER'S LOVE TIP
When love is in mint condition, sacrifice won't feel like sacrifice at all. It will actually be a pleasure to defer to the other part.

Grace

G race is a powerful program with diverse functions. After all, "grace" can be a blessing said before a meal. You can possess grace or adorn yourself in gracious fashion. On the other hand, it is by the grace of God that we "live and move and have our being" (Acts 17:28 NIV). And one can choose to be gracious or grace someone with her presence. Grace can be a noun or a verb, but it will always be a blessing.

What Grace Does

It Redeems People
The major function of grace is that it redeems people. When You extend grace to your partner, he is redeemed (and vice versa). When you offer grace, you are able to look beyond others' faults to see their needs, even when their words or actions are negative. This is grace operating at its peak.

It Sees People with Love
Grace considers the other person through the eyes of love, eliminating negative expectations and assumptions. If You are practicing grace, You disregard your partner's disappointing behavior and instead think, *Hmm, he must be having a bad day. This is not the normal behavior of the one I love.*

It Exchanges Strength for Weakness

Grace offers strength to cover the faults and weaknesses of the other person. You exchange your own strength for his weakness in order to cover any offenses that might result from his failings.

It Is Self-Powered

Grace runs on its own. It does not depend on the goodness of others or the kindness of strangers. It is grounded in the GOD piece and is consistent in its function long after other programs have run out of juice.

In other words, when You are operating in grace, You do not succumb to others' bad behavior. Grace maintains a higher level of love. It fuels the relationship with hope because it chooses to focus on the good qualities of the other person. Grace is fully operational even when—*especially* when—the other person is being impossible to live with. Grace knows there's a better person underneath and cheers him on.

It Covers Sin

The Manufacturer's Manual says, "Above all, love each other deeply, because love covers over a multitude of sins" (1 Pet. 4:8 NIV). Grace enables true love to work and allows You to look past things your partner does that offend You. With grace, You aren't judgmental or condemning.

Does that mean that practicing grace is automatic and easy? No. Grace might require counting to ten, talking to yourself, walking away for a moment until the smoke clears—doing whatever You need to do to get back to the good part of the relationship.

Practicing grace can be the hardest thing to do in a love relationship. When your partner fails to live up to your expectations, your love for him will be unduly strained. Repeated disappointment in your mate can cause You to stall emotionally and eventually lead You to believe that You are no longer in love.

Grace is able to override disappointment by choosing to continue believing the best of the other person. With grace, You don't go into denial over issues that need to be addressed; but You do remain committed to strengthening your love for him.

It Provides the Lifeblood of Your Relationship

Grace goes against the human grain and keeps You loving long after others have given up. It is a partner of mercy, which is the lifeblood of every love connection.

You have the capacity to empower your partner by granting him grace. Sometimes all any of us needs is the knowledge that someone loves us enough to accept us as we are, flaws and all. Grace says, "I love you anyway."

It Empowers the Struggling Partner

Grace actually empowers your partner. Your quiet acceptance strengthens your partner to rise to the occasion and be the person he should be. As water seeks its own level, people generally will do less if less is expected of them. However, in the face of love that is extended graciously, your partner decides to be a better person for You.

I think of Jesus sitting at a well, talking with a certain woman who no doubt had her fair share of criticism and judgment (see John 4). The woman had married five husbands, one after the other, and was then living with a man. Her actions made for juicy gossip. Can you imagine what her neighbors had to say?

We don't know if these men had all left her or died. I'm sure the women who longed to have even one husband were evil to her. All the married women probably clung to their spouses a little tighter when she was in the vicinity. Suffice it to say she was popular, but not in a good way.

But Jesus, the Rabbi, the Redeemer, chose to sit there and ask this woman for water, making her feel worthwhile. Free of judgment, though He knew everything about her, He went straight to the heart of her need and offered what she was really looking for: love that would not fail or run dry. He empowered her that day to break out of her routine of searching for love in all the wrong places and embrace her own worth, no longer needing affirmation or validation from some man. She ended up evangelizing the city, so passionate was she about the One who had given her newfound love and worth.

When You choose to remove pressure, judgment, and criticism from the relationship, your partner will have no excuse for not doing the right thing. Still, grace helps You to allow for failure because You understand humanity's limitations. Grace empowers You to be kind in the midst of your partner's bad behavior because your self-worth is not dependent on his being your all and all.

> Grace is a program that is complete in itself; therefore, regardless of what anyone else does, says, does not do, or does not say, it continues to function (see Eph. 2:8).

This is the mystery of love—that You can reach past the failures, offenses, and disappointments of the one who let You down to touch the part of him that is good and true and perfect. In that moment, You ignite love all over again and both partners have another chance to do the right thing. Grace says, "I understand."

The Power of Grace

Grace lifts your partner to higher ground. It equips both parts to operate at their best by giving them what they need to keep going even in extreme circumstances. You will know that You have mastered grace when it kicks into high gear at the same time the MAN least expects or deserves forgiveness or a second chance. It will be your opportunity to catch him off-guard with a gentleness that convicts him to shape up and do the right thing. Can we do any less? Look at the Manufacturer's Manual (see Rom. 5:8)!

Grace is a powerful program because it overrides and deletes guilt. This is what God utilizes with us. Guilt releases the shame virus, which forces people into hiding. Of course this hiding paralyzes communication, creating distance for as long as the couple avoids addressing the offensive issue. Depending on the stamina of the two partners, this period could be very long. Since distance will weaken passion, and passion is a necessary part of the relationship, it is important to immediately delete avoidance behavior. It is death to the love unit.

You must be willing to look past the offense to say what God would say: "'Come now, let us reason together,' says the Lord. 'Though your sins are like scarlet, they shall be as white as snow'" (Isa. 1:18 NIV). There it is—grace offering restoration to the injured party because grace understands that someone hurts You because he hurts. Offense, in a sense, is a cry for help. It is evidence that someone is so trapped in his pain he is blinded by it and is flailing to find his way out.

Grace helps You feel your partner's pain and seek to mend and restore rather than add friction that could impair his ability to function. This is true not just in the love relationship but in any encounter You may have.

From the rude salesclerk to the irritable coworker to hypersensitive friends (oops—I know you don't have any of those!), the principle is the same: hurt people hurt other people. It is a knee-jerk reaction to pain. To stop in that moment and extend grace even when your partner is undeserving is the most powerful thing You can do.

And to go a step further and ask, "Is everything all right?" can completely diffuse an approaching explosion. Communicating that You see something worth salvaging in the MAN gives You the power You need to get past any outburst or offense that can threaten the love connection.

In order to give grace, You must be a recipient of grace yourself. If You do not receive grace, You will fool yourself into believing that You are all that, making You self-righteous and judgmental. It is important to note that no one is perfect, not even You. If You understand this, You will find it easier to extend grace.

Amazing, Everlasting Grace

Remember the song "We Shall Not Be Moved"? That about sums it up. Grace helps You remain steady. It helps You adapt to every situation with poise. Relentlessly kind in all circumstances, You will be able to maintain your composure and remain gracious under fire. Grace will keep You from demeaning others who may upset You because You are operating on a higher level of understanding and love.

Grace takes its power directly from the GOD part. Without being properly aligned with this main Source of power, grace cannot function. It must be activated daily to perform consistently. If it becomes deactivated, serious damage can occur. The only way to forgive the unforgivable, love the unlovable, and reason with the unreasonable is to utilize the grace that the GOD piece extends to all connected parts, extensions, and programs.

Grace makes a gentle appeal and lends dignity to everyone involved. It inspires by example. Exchanging grace sparks a flow of passion that fuels the love connection, which can result in love growing stronger if both partners choose to engage without reserve. Then love will always work.

INSIDER'S LOVE TIP
Gracious living will always bring more grace to You. It will empower You to keep your head when all around You everyone is losing theirs and capsizing their relationships in the midst of the drama. Last but not least, grace will always leave You looking your best regardless of how You feel.

Forgiveness

J ust because you've mastered grace, don't fool yourself into believing that You can be gracious without forgiving. You may be a class act, but the act will only be as deep as the heart of the action. You can be gracious to people and still hold them captive in a prison of unforgiveness. This is where your acts of kindness can actually become a burden to others because deep in their psyches, they are made to feel unworthy of all your niceness. Eventually, You will agree, and the love connection will be in danger of exploding. Forgiveness is one of the most critical programs in maintaining the love connection. Without this program, love will fail to operate for any significant amount of time. The MAN will fail You. It's a brutal fact. No matter how in love You are, no matter how much of a smooth operator he may be, his humanity will shock your love circuits sooner or later by disappointing or offending You.

Actually, his failure is not a terrible thing. It reminds You to make sure your connection to the GOD part is secure at all times because all other parts and programs are imperfect. Only the GOD piece will operate consistently.

Vital Help against the Unforgiveness Virus

Your inability to cut your partner some slack could cost You the love connection. If forgiveness is not installed and used repeatedly, bitterness could clog your system.

> You will have to decide: do You want to be right or do You
> want the relationship? Sometimes standing on principle
> leaves You standing alone, or worse yet, slowly drowning in
> the bitter waters of unforgiveness.

Bitterness is hard to remove and can cause major corrosion to vital
parts such as the HEART and MIND. Unforgiveness is a slow-working
virus that is not initially apparent. It subtly begins to slow down the flow
of love without either You or your partner being aware of its presence—
until the cold distance between you comes to light. Unforgiveness is the
greatest killer of passion in a relationship. (If this has occurred in your
relationship, please refer to the Troubleshooting section of this guide.)

It is crucial to the life of your relationship to deal with each situation as its own new experience. Do You want to pay for someone
else's failures—your spouse's ex-girlfriend or mother's mistreatment
of him? Absolutely not, right? So don't impose that burden on the
one You love either. Learn not to hoard past offenses. These are viruses that can jam your system. The Manufacturer is adamant about
keeping all circuits clear so love can flow freely.

When You are the offended party, You must utilize aforementioned
grace to continue functioning individually as a part. This is as much for
your sake as it is for the relationship. Why? Your refusal to exercise mercy
will affect your personal makeup. You are wired to imitate the GOD part,
and the GOD part is not thin-skinned or easily offended. Should You
allow unforgivenesss to become a habit, You will develop severe problems in your mind-set and eventually in all of your relationships.

Remember what the Manufacturer's Manual tells us about forgiveness: "Then Peter came to Jesus and asked, 'Lord, how many times
shall I forgive my brother when he sins against me? Up to seven
times?' Jesus answered, 'I tell you, not seven times, but seventy-
seven times'" (Matt. 18:21–22 NIV).

How to Address an Offense

The instructions for addressing offense are direct. We will look at these step by step. In the meantime, know that the Manual does not recommend that You harbor your hurt. Going into denial only delays your response, causing You to act out inappropriately at another time. It also enables the offender to continue offending You.

1. First, Examine Your Own HEART
Consider why You are offended or hurt. Is it possible that what he said was true? In what ways did his actions affect You and why? Is it simply personal inconvenience or a greater issue?

2. Approach the Offender
Never confront someone in anger. Formulate your thoughts, and approach the MAN expecting only the best of him. Remember, anytime You respond out of anger, hurt, or fear, You will say and/or do the wrong thing and, in most cases, further damage your relationship. Explaining how You felt rather than pointing the finger is usually an effective way to get to the heart of the matter.

Most of the time, You will be surprised to discover that the MAN did not mean what You thought he meant at all. This will diffuse the entire situation. When left to run its course through the imagination, an offense can destroy every good feeling for your beloved. Therefore, if your partner offends You, go to him and, speaking the truth in love, expose the offense and get rid of it (see Matt. 18:15).

3. Get Help If You Need It
If his response does not satisfy You, feel free to enlist the help of a mediator to walk both of you through the misunderstanding. This option comes straight from the Manufacturer's Manual (see Matt. 18:16–17).

4. Forgive Regardless

Unfortunately, from time to time, the other person might not get the point You were trying to convey. Forgive anyway (see Prov. 19:11). In this case, your love will have to stand in the gap and cover the offense (see Prov. 17:9), while You release your partner to God.

You can't overlook the importance of forgiveness because ultimately, if You let the offense crowd your mind, it will affect your discernment. An offended person has relinquished control to the person who offended him or her. An out of control person is like an unfortified city—open and vulnerable to anything, including influences toward wrong actions and reactions (see Prov. 25:28).

Note: Forgiving the offender does not require that You stay in a threatening situation. In cases of abuse or adultery, if your partner shows no repentance, I advise You to seek counseling in the interest of getting to the root of the problem and finding a workable solution. If You are in physical danger, by all means, get out of the house.

If your partner is neither amenable to counsel nor cooperative with your request that he change his destructive behavior, You might have to take a harder line for the sake of self-preservation—especially if children are involved—by seeking a permanent separation.

To remain in such an environment consistently overtaxes your capacity to forgive and can impair your health on all levels. Such an environment can cause permanent damage to your spirit, your emotions, and even your physical being.

Take care. Forgive if possible, but don't dance with danger.

Drop Unrealistic Expectations

In order to keep forgiveness active in your relationship, You need to dismantle unrealistic expectations. In many cases, You set yourself up to be offended by insisting on rules that are not possible for your partner to keep. This results in your gauging the love of the other person by the wrong criteria. If the other person does not live up to your expectations, You do not feel loved because he did not stick to and fulfill your "list."

Down with lists! A list is neither realistic nor fair to your partner, as he will never know the full extent of your list. And just because it's *your* list does not make it the bottom line on anything. To insist that people line up with your expectations is a little like playing God, don't you think? Even our perfect GOD understands that as humans, we will fail, and He extends His forgiveness, along with the invitation to exercise our free will.

For YOU and your partner to experience a greater flow of love, YOU must lay aside the list and replace it with an agreement about what is required for you both to love at your peak. We will discuss communication later, but for now suffice it to say that neither of you has ESP and you both have to allow for failure.

The real beauty of forgiveness is that it strengthens the bond between you because you've weathered something together and overcome it. Until this occurs, most relationships remain superficial because they have never been tested. Therefore, never balk at disagreements and offenses. Embrace them and use them to strengthen your connection. This is what maintenance is all about.

INSIDER'S LOVE TIP
Forgiveness is the least expensive program in the love unit. If, however, pride overrides forgiveness, it can appear to be the most costly.

Faith

The faith program is an essential part of maintenance. Without the expectation of anything good coming out of your efforts, You will not be motivated to apply yourself to the work involved to keep love going. When faith is broken, the work will stop, and the relationship will stall.

Faith is reliance on the power of the commitment of the two main parts to continue functioning in the relationship. Without the assurance that your partner is as invested in the relationship as You are, it is difficult to do the work to keep love up and running.

Aspects of Faith

Faith Believes

What You believe about the possibilities of the relationship as well as what You believe about your partner will affect how your love works. The rise in prenuptial agreements suggests that faith in love going the distance has hit an all-time low. People want to protect themselves "just in case" things don't work out.

Though I'm not aware of any research being done on how a prenup affects a couple's psyche, I think it's safe to suggest that it could cause two people to begin a significant journey with a huge question mark. For the person asked to sign the agreement, this question is always lurking in her spirit: *Does this mean he intends to get rid of me at some point?* Or the other thought: *Just what does this person think I intend to do to him? What does this say about how he views my character?* These thoughts can be slow poison to a relationship.

So how does one set the stage for mutual trust and adoration in a world where life happens? People bail out of love. Bad health happens. Money issues devastate relationships. The list of all the things that can assault and destroy a love connection is a long one. Yet love can prevail in the midst of trying circumstances. It comes down to commitment.

Faith Means No "Out" Clause

Singles, make up your mind on this one before approaching the altar, and you will be ahead of the game. Let's back up to before the altar for a moment. Before we can progress to serious commitment many of us destroy potential relationships based on our insecurities, wondering if a truly committed relationship is something that can really happen for us. We must believe that having the love we want and need is totally possible. With that faith comes the commitment to doing whatever we need to do to make the relationship a reality, which leads us to the place of saying "I do."

Faithfulness says that no matter what happens, divorce is not an option. This is definitely a "till death do us part" mind-set at work. Remember, emotions follow decisions. If there is no "out" clause in your mind, heart, or spirit, you create determination to work through whatever changes come.

These were the vows spoken in church, in front of witnesses: "For richer, for poorer, in sickness and in health, till death do us part." People say these words, but do they truly consider them? Broken vows destroy the work of our hands and hearts (see Eccl. 5:4–6). The things we build are devastated when we don't adhere to the promises we make. The wonderful home, the family unit, the children, and all that goes into the making of a marriage suffer when promises made are not promises kept.

All of this is a matter of faith. We adhere to what we believe. We abandon anything we have no faith in.

Faith Means Hope

The Manufacturer's Guide tells us that faith is all about believing in what you cannot see (see Heb. 11:1). Again, if You are single, just because You don't have a relationship right now doesn't mean You never will, that something is wrong with You or that You are unlovable. Consider this season of waiting to be a delicate time during which the Master Manufacturer Himself is aligning all the right components to create the best product imaginable—the love You really need, which will be good *to* You and *for* You. Remember, You can only take hold of what You envision through the eyes of your belief. Seeing the invisible leaves You open and ready to embrace the endless possibilities instead of shutting them down.

For those who are married already, You must be able to envision your partner through the lens of positive expectancy. Faith sometimes hangs on little more than a wing and a prayer. Will your partner ever become the person You want him to be? Many ask this question after marrying people they decided they would capture now and fix later, or after discovering things about their spouses they did not notice during the courtship.

Still, those who endure to the end usually get the reward of the marriage they want. To bail prematurely is like working a job all week, quitting before payday, and never receiving your check because You didn't believe the company had the money to pay You. Imagine your mortification when You discover that all the other people who stayed got paid! I recall entering my name in a drawing once to win a PDA I really wanted. However, I didn't really believe I would win. My attitude was, "Oh well, I never win anything. Why should this time be different?" So I didn't hang around for the drawing. An hour later, I walked past the stand where the promotion had been held. Guess what? I had won! But I couldn't receive my prize because you had to be present when your name was called. Aaagh! Many of us live life and approach relationships this way. The end of unbelief or lack of faith is that You will never be able to claim the prize You couldn't imagine was yours for the taking. Moral of the story? Stick it out and have faith.

Many who have amazing relationships with their spouses have said the marriage they now share is not what they started with. It was by persevering through the ups and downs that beauty emerged. Faithfulness, expressed through continual hope, definitely has its rewards.

Faith in your relationship, in your partner, and in the ability of God to keep what You cannot keep yourself will help You stand firm even if the foundation is shaking. The Manufacturer's Manual says, "So guard yourself in your spirit, and do not break faith with the wife [husband] of your youth" (Mal. 2:15 NIV).

You already know that not every day of your life, whether You have a relationship or not, will be a frolic in the park. There will be seasons of change, shake-ups, and breakdowns. A committed love relationship can help You weather these things better *or* make them even more difficult. It all depends on You and your commitment to faithfulness.

Faith Calls for Focus
Faith asks You to examine yourself because You are the only one You have control over in the equation. Through the eyes of faith, You see the big picture of your relationship without overlooking the work that will be needed to see that vision come to light.

Looking into the eyes of the one You love, You see endless possibilities and the promise of an amazing relationship. As You fix your eyes on the vision inspired by your faith, everything within You will line up to walk toward what You see.

While learning to drive when I was sixteen, I had a lot of difficulty keeping the car straight on the road until the driving instructor told me where to fix my focus. Without focus, I was weaving all over the road, but when I honed in on where I was headed, I was able to stabilize the wheel and keep the car on track.

Where is your focus? A bride who is determined to be two sizes smaller on her wedding day will let the vision of herself with a trim waist in a beautiful dress keep her on the diet. What You see is what You will have.

So what do You see? A rich relationship that feeds and empowers both of you? If You see nothing, You will do nothing to build and solidify your relationship. You must do the work to build what You hope for in your relationship—by faith.

Faith in Whom?

Now here's the caveat. You must set your faith in the right place to avoid disappointment. All your faith cannot rest in your partner, because in his humanity, he will fail You. You must place your faith in God operating inside of your beloved to keep him connected to You.

With your faith in God, You are empowered to give your all unconditionally, trusting that GOD will protect the link between you. You've got to have faith to feed the relationship everything it needs to grow. Faith empowers You to be vulnerable, honest, giving, and passionate without reserve (see Mark 9:23).

If You do not believe that what You have to give will be received, You will not be free to give. The saying has long been "No pain, no gain," but I offer You a different motto: when it comes to making love work, "No faith, no gain" is more appropriate.

No one takes a risk without faith. You would not jump if You did not believe the bungee cord would keep You from plummeting to your death. You exercise faith a thousand times a day without thinking about it. You cross the street believing the cars at the light will stop. You get on a plane, buckle your safety belt, and fall asleep in your seat believing You will wake up safe and sound at your desired destination. You eat food at restaurants cooked by strangers and believe it will not poison You. You take leaps of faith every day.

You must take the leap to love by faith, to cast yourself into the arms of your partner, believing he will catch and embrace your offerings, and into the arms of God, knowing and trusting that God is able to keep safe what your partner can't.

YOU also hold out your arms by faith to catch what YOU pray your partner will offer YOU. To open your heart and allow another to enter takes faith. To invite him to stay and believe he will also takes faith. To believe he will not pilfer and destroy the contents of your heart takes even greater faith.

We are instructed again to imitate God, who believes the best of us in the midst of our failings. Through the eyes of love, God sees us as flawless (see Psalm 103:12), even in our most abhorrent state. He dares to cheer us on, believing that we will ultimately be transformed into a glorious reflection of Him as we yield to His love. This is the same hope each of us must have in order for love to work.

YOU must dare to believe that as YOU pour yourself out for the benefit of your partner, he will be transformed by your love, and YOU by his. By faith, you continue to operate all programs conducive to love, believing that your love can go the distance. Dare to love fearlessly and faithfully, because perfect love will completely delete fear and override any other virus that might threaten its operation, and that is the greatest evidence of faith there is.

INSIDER'S LOVE TIP
What YOU desire has to be greater than your fear in order for YOU to press past it. Faith is fueled by your passion to embrace your desire. Love is not blind; it simply has faith.

Perseverance

The Manufacturer's Manual tells us that the race is won not by the fastest among us but by those who endure to the end (see 2 Tim. 4:7). Nothing less can be said about love. Many make the initial connection, but few keep the current strong until the end. When the first sparks fly, chemistry abounds, but eventually it fizzles out, requiring both You and the Man to get down to the daily business of maintaining a working love relationship. This is where perseverance comes in.

If forgiveness is functioning properly in the relationship and integrity can be grounded in your love unit, there is a great chance that love can be restored to its initial levels. In some cases, You will find that defragmenting and rebooting can actually strengthen your love and leave it in better condition than at the onset. If You and your partner can use disappointments to clarify where your relationship needs improvement, setbacks can actually work to your benefit. This is called refurbished love.

Your love will be refurbished only if both of you are willing to disassemble all of your previous expectations to expose and tear out the damaged areas of the relationship. You must submit these areas to the Manufacturer so He can repair them effectively or upgrade them. Anything that endangers the love connection, whether it be other people, habits, or attitudes, must be removed before you as a unit can move forward.

Five Steps to Perseverance

What is the secret to persevering in the love program? Another word for perseverance is steadfastness: remaining on course, maintaining a smooth and steady path toward the victory You desire in your relationship. You move with determination toward the love You want to have permanently downloaded and captured in your love unit.

There are five steps to this operation, which we will approach one by one. In some ways, the following instructions will seem like a recap of the former maintenance steps, but they are necessary to clarify your strategy for keeping up your love unit.

Step #1: Commit to the Commitment

Several years back, the world watched a runner fall on the Olympic track. It became evident that something was seriously wrong as he attempted to get up, regain his footing, and finish the race. As he hopped his way down the track, his father joined him on the field, supporting him as he made his way in agony across the finish line. Of course, he didn't win a medal, but he won the admiration of everyone watching. This athlete was a perfect picture of commitment.

To determined athletes, quitting does not compute. They live, breathe, eat, and dream of winning. It is this vision that makes them steadfast in their pursuit of the goal. Both parts in the love unit must have the same type of ferocious focus. You must be consumed by the thought of installing, maintaining, saving, and completing your love program with aplomb. You must make up your MIND to optimize your operating system and be open to new and improved programs that keep everything in perfect running order.

As I've said, it is normal for feelings of love to fluctuate. Your emotions on any given day are not an accurate gauge for deciding whether You should keep or discard the relationship. You must hold yourself accountable to something higher than your wishy-washy feelings, the effects of outward stimuli, or restlessness.

You must be accountable first to God and then to your partner, who will hold You to the vows You made. "To have and to hold forever" must be more than a good intention. These are covenant words. Those who are still dating should covenant to always be honest about your intentions toward each other, to respect and honor each other as you take the time to solidify your connection.

A covenant is more substantial than a contract. A contract has conditions that can expire if terms are not kept, but a covenant has no expiration date and is binding for life. It can be severed only should one partner die. Note: there is a difference between your dying and your feelings of love dying. As a matter of fact, You should know that true love never dies (see 1 Cor. 13:8).

The best relationships I know of have faced trauma and conflict and survived. Every love unit should have a surge protector to equalize the two main parts should their circuits become overloaded from stress, difficulty, and all the things that threaten their love unit.

Trouble-free love exists only in the movies . . . but it doesn't really exist even there! Every writer knows that a good script contains conflict. Boy chases girl. Girl resists boy's advances. Boy wins girl. Boy loses girl. Boy gets girl back. Hooray! We love to watch it but we don't like to live it.

You will have to make lots of adjustments for the life of your love unit. Some things will fall into place easily. Others will take a lifetime to adjust to. Love is a journey full of false starts, surges, errors, crashes, operational failures, and magnificent breakthroughs. Decide to endure together.

Step #2: Keep Your Head
A friend shared with me her strategy for maintaining her marriage. She intellectually understood that every day would present its own threats to her happy little love nest, so she decided to take an offensive approach rather than run around putting out fires after they occurred. Every

morning when she woke up she prayed, "Lord, show me what I need to watch out for today and give me the wisdom to have the right response."

Wow! This is huge. Use your head and your prayer life. These two things will keep your love unit balanced when anything threatens the stability of the unit or threatens to shake up your operating system. Don't get rocked by what your invisible enemy, Satan (remember him?), throws at your relationship. Remember, he hates love units that run effectively. His mission is to steal, kill, and destroy your love program so that You can't function. Don't let it happen!

Love requires You to use your mind as much as your heart. Remember, your emotions will follow your decisions. You must intellectually recognize the things that endanger the productivity and health of your relationship and make conscientious choices to guard it with all that is within You.

Protecting your relationship includes avoiding anything that can be destructive to your love: strong friendships with the opposite sex, repeated offenses to your partner, dishonesty, habits that affect the security of the household (financial irresponsibility, abuse, unresolved tensions—You know what I'm talking about). The bottom line is this: do not allow yourself to be swayed by outward influences that don't feed and nurture the love unit.

Step #3: Pay Attention

I'm a bit perplexed by how many love units over the age of fifty are crashing or quitting altogether. The seminars I lead are filled with weeping women who've spent at least half their lives with men who suddenly decided to leave. I ask the same question every time: What happened? At first, my question is met with a blank stare, hunched shoulders and a weary sounding, "I don't know; I didn't see it coming." Upon further questioning, many admit that their men hinted at unhappiness, but they didn't take the hints seriously, not realizing the depth of discontent their husbands felt. The women grew distracted by family life, and they shifted their priorities away from their husbands. These distractions and shifts started a slow virus of resentment that led to ultimate failure.

In some cases, the circumstances were reversed and the MAN was no longer what the woman felt she needed or wanted. This happens when we don't take the time to do regular virus scans or reboot our relationships to reconfigure them to the most current settings in our partners' HEARTS. It's important to pay attention to your own HEART as well as the MAN's and be willing to have the hard discussions as part of your maintenance program.

A transparent heart along with accountability to God and your partner form the greatest foundation for securing your relationship. Do not turn away from the subtle warnings, inner promptings, or loud cries for help your partner may emit. Denial is not a river in Egypt; it is a dangerous country that harbors failure, desperation, and death. Don't go there. Face your stuff, and get rid of what is not working in your relationship.

Do not point fingers and cast blame. Remember that when YOU point one finger at someone, three are pointing back at YOU. Take responsibility for your part of the dance. Even though the truth may hurt, it is the light that reveals the path to where YOU ultimately want to go (see Psalm 119:105). Follow it and embrace it for all it's worth.

Step #4: Do the Work

I have a confession to make. I hate my physical trainer. Every other morning at 7 AM he stands over me like a drill sergeant, putting me through the paces of exercise. I hate exercise, but I want to look fit and trim. My ego and my need to be in good health override my disdain for physical exertion. So I make the decision to do the work it will take to look and feel good.

The same holds true if YOU want your love to look and feel good. Your love unit will not function at its own discretion; it waits to be programmed and run by YOU. It will only output what YOU input.

When YOU decide to do the work required to make love flourish, your satisfaction will be worth all the sweat and tears. Work to become the best person YOU can be for the sake of your partner. YOU cannot get lazy in love. What it took to attract the MAN must be maintained to keep love intact.

You should never dishonor your partner by behaving as if he is not worth the trouble of being your best for him. Be your best for him, but also be your best for You. This will keep your self-esteem at an all-time high, which will only make you more desirable to your partner.

Being your best means doing the work to keep yourself up physically. A friend of mine once said when people gain weight after getting married, they should be arrested for false advertising. After all, he bought one package and now had an entirely different one! I told him he should make some concessions for wear and tear, especially since it inevitably works both ways—at least it does for most.

Also do the work to become more caring. In a recent movie set in a rehab clinic, the patients were told that only after they were able to grow a plant and take care of a pet successfully would they be ready for a relationship. Why? Because both the plant and the pet required consistent nurturing.

Love will wither if it is not nurtured. It needs to be stimulated outwardly, nurtured inwardly, and guarded from all things that endanger its life. In other words, You must do the work to remain attractive and stimulating. You must weed out anything that hinders your love from growing stronger.

All this being said, when it is truly love, the work won't feel like work at all (see Gen. 29:20).

Step #5: Apply Yourself to Your Ministry

Singles and marrieds listen up—if You didn't know before, You need to know now. Marriage, despite what You may have been told, is a privilege and a high calling. It is the premier unit on the planet. Not all get the privilege of operating this great machine, so ownership should never be taken for granted. It is a job requiring great skill and command of all things technical and substantive. But most of all, it is a ministry.

Yes, love is a ministry. You have been called to serve your partner, pray for your partner, and die to self for the sake of your partner. You are called to stand in the gap for him, to cover him, to feed him spiritually, emotionally, and physically, and to administer your touch to the mind, body, and soul of the MAN with whom YOU desire to make love work.

Your ministry of love is your life calling—above all things, including your career and other relationships—once you've said "I do." To give of yourself over and over again until there is nothing left of YOU means that, if your partner is also giving, the two of you will become one in spirit.

Oneness is the highest level love operates on (see Eccl. 4:12). In oneness, the two of you are so intricately interwoven that separate parts are no longer distinguishable. The Accessories portion of this guide should clarify why oneness is crucial to your relationship. Suffice it to say for now that unity equals strength. Once you've placed yourself in permanent commitment mode, your first calling is to your partner.

Your partner's choosing to disengage does not demagnetize YOU, devalue YOU, shut down your program, or brand YOU a failure if YOU know YOU gave your all.

It's all about maintenance, y'all. Should YOU and your partner decide to allow love to run its full course, pace yourself. Those who make it to the end have mastered pacing; they never overexert their units with short blasts of electricity that could overload their circuits. They also know when to rely on auxiliary power, exchanging strength for strength, while recharging their batteries to sustain their love for the long term.

In permanent love connections, frequent tune-ups are highly recommended. Information on where your love can be serviced is at the back of this guide.

INSIDER'S LOVE TIP
What You decide to invest in your love unit can make the difference between love's being a duty or an exciting adventure that gives You a reason to rise every morning with great expectancy and joy.

Winning couples continue operating at full power until they've completed their alignment in a strong show of optimization, counting all the perseverance well worth the prize: love realized.

4

Maintenance:
Long-term

Passion

LOVE

You've seen it in the movies, and you've probably even experienced it: the heat that burns in the eyes of the one who is totally smitten by You. Invisible but potent, it takes your breath away and ignites your desire for the MAN. It makes a woman step outside her comfort zone and walk on air. She is transported by the sheer force of passion.

Passion can be like a drug, addictive in nature, but it is also a powerful program for igniting and engaging two people. Passion is the precursor to satisfying intimacy (more on that in the Accessories portion of this guide). Passion is the desire, while intimacy refers to the physical act or emotional expression of what You feel. You can be intimate without being physical, and it is passion that drives You to pursue deep intimacy with your partner.

Passion, however, must be fueled or it can dissipate. You must focus your passion as well as reignite it time and time again throughout the love relationship. It is one of the initiators of the dating relationship, but it is also what will jump-start your relationship again and again. Like fire, it can run wild and wreak havoc or, when focused in the right direction, add ardor to your love that compels You and the MAN to come together in an explosive celebration of love.

Warning: Passion can easily give way to obsession if not channeled through the GOD part. Though passion is good, You need to maintain balance in the midst of your zeal.

Passion's Purpose

Why would the Manufacturer install such a volatile program in You and the MAN? Because passion is needed to override fear, selfishness, or the reserve that your system might be harboring. Without passion, the MAN's presence would feel like an intrusion or invasion of your private space. This feeling would trigger negative reactions that repel the very connection You crave.

Something has to compel You to give yourself to someone in this way. Once a permanent connection has been made, there is no more You. Your personal universe of "I" and "me" must now embrace the concept of "we" and "us." This is what will move You from dating to committing yourself to a partner on a permanent basis. Selfishness must be conquered during the dating process for the relationship to move forward in a positive and productive manner. This can be a scary pursuit if You are not driven by passion.

> Passion creates a longing for your partner that is greater than your fear of what You think You stand to lose in the relationship.

The desire to be with your partner overwhelms your reservations and compels You to take the leap into love. It is this feeling, coupled with all You share during the courtship period, that gets You to seal the deal or form a steady if not permanent link.

Passion is not just sexual in nature. The exchange between the two of you on every level—intellectual, spiritual, physical, and emotional—ignites passion and causes You and the MAN to trade positive energy that is mutually transforming. It is the friction of minds, ideas, and commonalities along with the quirky, unique features of both of you that cause the sparks to fly between you.

Keep Passion Fed

The sad truth is that passion will dissipate if not consistently fed (i.e., regularly upgraded). So how do You feed passion and reignite it once you've entered a committed relationship?

Keep Your Identity

It is up to both partners to maintain the authenticity of who they are within the confines of their relationship. This is what makes their love unique and stimulating. Blending into oneness does not mean losing your unique features; You merely expand them to include the other person. Look at it this way: two puzzle pieces fit together to complete a picture without losing their shape.

Keep Dating

After many a MAN commits to a girlfriend and she becomes his wife, he finds her replaced by someone who no longer resembles the woman he fell in love with. All of a sudden, she isn't as vibrant and interesting as she once was. She has traded her spiked heels for wife and mommy shoes and forgotten the dance of flirtation that once attracted him. If You are preparing for marriage, commit now to keep the courtship alive after marriage to avoid having to troubleshoot later. (More on this in the next section.)

Keep Each Other Guessing

Falling into predictable patterns and mediocrity will cause passion to fizzle big-time. In other words, you've got to mix it up. The chase must continue even after the connection has been solidified.

The chase takes place naturally during courtship when each part is still working to steer the other toward engagement, but it can fade to black during marriage. Both of you must continue to grow so that you will always be discovering something new about each other. Stirring fascination and curiosity are sure measures for keeping passion alive. Not only must you be interested, you must also be interesting.

Baiting and catching, the delightful tease and the fun of being caught all over again keep romance fresh and passion alive between two people in love.

Use the Little Things

It's the little things that ignite passion, from a light touch to the lift of a brow to a conspiratorial smile. Nurture passion by setting the mood for it in your personal space. Tantalize all his senses with perfume, food, music, a great outfit, a habitual touch that triggers feelings of romance. Keep in mind that not all touch has to be sexual; touch is a wonderful way of creating a sense of familiarity and affection with your loved one. A whisper, a sigh, a motion—only You will know what stirs your partner. Pay close attention and then work your stuff.

Singles Beware

In the courtship stage, it is crucial to harness and focus passion because it can work against You just as it can work for You. Passion as a focus can decimate a love unit. When harnessed, though, it can produce positive tension that accelerates engagement.

In order to harness passion, You must rein in your thoughts. They cannot be allowed to roam unfettered. Remember, your body will follow your MIND, so discipline yourself to refocus when You find your thoughts wandering into areas that stir up your hormones or begin to build fires You will not be able to extinguish. Also, use physical activity (exercise, walking, dancing) to release tension and energy. Those who fail to expend their energy will either implode or utilize their passion in ways that are detrimental to themselves as well as the love unit. Just remember: passion can feed love or kill it. Both passion and love need to be handled with care as they are both volatile.

Love does not just happen. Passion doesn't either. Once you've achieved a permanent link, plan for it. Ignite it and fan the flame—obtain regular upgrades—until the heat fuses you together in an embrace that compares to no other. That keeps love working.

INSIDER'S LOVE TIP
Never play with passion. Respect its power.

Rituals

Far too many love connections fall apart because of a lack of activity. Far too many relationships fade to black because romance gets filed away once two people have committed to each other at the altar.

The romantic habits that a couple practice initially sometimes get lost as both partners get used to each other. Maybe he no longer holds the door for You; maybe You don't say "thank you" as often. Maybe you've stopped dating—setting time aside to reconnect romantically and emotionally. The fact is, those rituals you performed early in the courtship period are foundational to your connection. They solidify the bond, giving both partners a familiar place to reengage and renew their commitment. This releases a fresh surge of power into the relationship.

Never take your relationship for granted. I think of a certain queen, Vashti in the book of Esther, who rested on her laurels and lost her crown. Her husband had been celebrating the expansion of his territories. The man had partied for six months when he remembered his beautiful wife and called her to come, dressed in her finery, for all his guests to see. She was in the midst of throwing her own party and refused.

Vashti would never have refused her husband's request at the beginning of their marriage, when she was still eager to please. The lesson? Never assume that You cannot be replaced. Girlfriend learned this lesson a little too late.

I don't think this was Vashti's first time upsetting the king. He rolled over too easily on the recommendation to have her removed from her throne. If she had been working her magic on him, I think he would have been more prone to forgive her.

Just because you have committed to each other does not guarantee the relationship will last if You and your partner don't work at maintaining a flow of love. Love is not sustained by chemistry; it is maintained by things like little romantic or endearing rituals—the behaviors that characterized the way you treated each other when you were still trying to win each other's love.

> It is those "little" things that establish strong connections and keep love grounded.

Note: Some of the following material will apply only to those who've engaged permanently (gotten married). Singles, read and learn!

Keeping Rituals Alive

Remember How You Used Time

Remember the initial part of your relationship? The two of you spent hours planning the times that You would spend together. You shifted schedules and changed your commitments so you could be with each other. Just because you are now either dating exclusively or married does not mean this should stop.

Time spent together intentionally should still be at the top of the priority list. You should set aside certain times just to connect: time to get in touch and, if necessary, get reacquainted. Strangers can't make love work.

Use Rituals to Jump-Start Romance

In nature, animals perform rituals. They go to the same places and do the same mating dances. These activities reestablish their roles as male and female and trigger their mating instincts.

There must be an order to romance, something that jump-starts it all over again. There is a way You and your partner approach each other, look at each other. When it comes to humans, all of this can fall to the wayside, but it shouldn't. There is an order to the universe that sets us all up to function at our best if the order is maintained.

Order creates consistency, allowing us to count on the same result each time. It gives You the power to respond in an appropriate fashion. Imagine if summer decided to come in winter months—what would happen to the world? Nature would be thrown completely out of whack and wreak certain destruction. The same thing happens when we don't interact in our relationships according to the Manufacturer's Manual. This does not mean things have to get boring or exclude variety. Winter comes regularly, but no snowflake is the same.

The Manufacturer is big on romance. With this in mind, You can program patterns into your relationship until these cues jump-start your mood for romance: playing certain songs, lighting candles, softening the lighting. Whatever gets You and your partner in gear, just maintain a pattern of consistency in the romance department.

Find the Wi-Fi Spot in Your Home

Just as "wi-fi" zones at airports, cafes, and hotels allow You to connect to the Internet, You must have a "hot spot" in your house that lets You achieve the ultimate connection. According to the rituals You set up, You will be able to identify the spot.

For many, this spot will be the bedroom, so let's start there.

The Ritual of Place: The Bedroom

Because rituals are really about keeping romance alive, let's begin with the bedroom. Maaaajor hot spot! This is the place that everyone races to (sometimes prematurely—see the Accessories part of this guide), but it is the first place to be misused after you've solidified your commitment. Suddenly, couples use it for everything *but* romance: watching television (isn't that supposed to be in the living room or den?), eating, talking on the phone, doing office work . . . You get my drift.

Your bedroom, before and after You have children, should be a sacred place: a place where the two of you reconnect and electricity is released to flow freely. Use these tips to keep this wi-fi spot humming.

Replace Fuses as Needed

The bedroom is the fuse box, the place where You and the Man reignite and refresh each other after the world has drained and exhausted you.

The Manufacturer highly recommends engaging in romance to the point of both parts being completely intoxicated with each other. He encourages the man in the relationship to be "ravished always with her love" (Prov. 5:19 asv). I believe this suggestion holds for both partners in the connection. This would imply that You, the woman, need to be turning him on and stirring things up and fanning the flame in response to his touch.

God does not want romantic interaction to stall or discontinue. As a matter of fact, the Manufacturer suggests that sexual intimacy should be avoided only for a time agreed upon by both parts for the purpose of fasting and prayer (see 1 Cor. 7:5).

In other words, keeping your physical relationship lively actually ignites some spiritual regeneration that makes you even better for each other. As always, your love connection will be only as great as your connection to the God part.

Set the Mood

You have to create an ambience of romance and intimacy. This has everything to do with setting and atmosphere. Your bedroom is the one place that should be free of everything that would distract you from each other. Decorate this room with care. The colors, the lighting, the furniture—only You know what looks like romance to You. Make sure that every sense is stimulated. Sight, sound, taste, smell, and touch.

All right—music, lights, action!

Other Wi-Fi Spots to Consider

The Kitchen

The bedroom is not the only wi-fi zone, although it should be the primary one for a couple, their secret garden of intimacy and exchange. The kitchen is also a hot spot.

From our childhood, the kitchen is a central spot for gathering. The feelings of warmth and security associated with this room follow us all the way through our adult lives. Just go to any party and notice where most people gather no matter how roomy the rest of the house may be. You've got it: the kitchen.

It is the place where communion occurs; it is warm, welcoming, and unpretentious. The kitchen allows people simply to be who they are, and that feels good.

The Dining Room

The dining room can be a wi-fi zone because some of the best communication takes place over a meal, feeding the soul as well as the body. This is where the distance created by going your separate ways during the workday is diminished and intimacy is reestablished. Small wonder that one of the first things Jesus did after dying, descending into hell, snatching the keys of hell and death away from Satan, leading captivity captive, and resurrecting was fix breakfast for His disciples.

Think of the magnitude of that action. After all the earth-shattering events of the previous few days, Jesus chose to nurture His discouraged and disillusioned disciples over a warm meal. 'Nuff said.

The Living (or Family) Room

The area where You relax after a long day is another place for couples to create warm feelings.

You will know and define your own "wi-fi" spots. As You locate them, You can designate rituals that You do in those areas: cooking something together in the kitchen, taking the time to snuggle and give each other a foot massage in your favorite big chair in the living room, or reading poetry or a good book to each other. Each room in your home can become a place where You achieve a strong, clear connection.

The Ritual of Touch

Touch is important because it establishes familiarity between two partners. It should trigger emotions that no one else's touch can. Your touch is your signature that leaves an indelible impression on the mind and spirit of your loved one. Touch establishes not only your presence but your connection in a crowded room. In some ways, it is a seal of ownership, reminding both of you whom you really belong to in social settings as well as private ones.

Touch not only reestablishes your connection to each other, but it also signals to others watching that your relationship is intact. Touch marks your territory in the presence of others and gives security to both partners. Should you be separated at a party, for instance, You are free to work the room, but make sure You do a walk-by to reconnect with your partner. Remember, there are always free-floating parts looking for someone to connect to. Never allow the MAN to be a freestanding fixture, thereby making him vulnerable to aggressive cruisers.

Whether You are single or married, touch is important. If you're single, though, and trying to maintain purity in your courtship, be honest with yourself and your partner about which lines should not be crossed. Touching and petting are not the same, so clarify and set the appropriate boundaries to help you honor each other before God. Unwrapping presents on Christmas or a birthday is much more exciting because of the anticipation. Premature discovery makes the day anticlimatic at best. The same is true of the physical aspect of your relationship.

The Ritual of Mental Engagement

The ritual of mental engagement is a powerful tool for keeping romance alive. The morning phone call, the noonday check-in, the last passionate kiss before closing your eyes, the card under the pillow, the rose left on the nightstand, the last lingering squeeze, the cup of coffee that stands waiting. Whatever the thing is that makes your partner smile and feel loved, You need to do it regularly.

Again, it is the little things, your little habits he misses when You are not there. These little things remain long after you've done them because, since You do them regularly, they are imbedded in your partner's heart and spirit.

Consistent behaviors, you see, help your partner feel secure about his connection to You (and vice versa). Consistent behaviors create patterns on your partner's soul that make all inappropriate outside contact feel like an intrusion. Positive, consistent actions will keep both of you feeling full and satisfied.

Remember, people seek other connections only when they are not "full filled"—filled to the point of fullness with the one who is supposed to be the period at the end of their sentence.

Rituals establish patterns in your relationship that ground both of you. Without this grounding, both partners are more open to interference from outside forces because they have set no boundaries to solidify their bond. Consistent romantic interaction reveals what your beloved can expect in the day to day and actually forms a buffer from unwanted outside attention.

Regularity becomes a sanctuary, a safe place that offers solace to both You and the MAN. It is in this place of comfort that your bond is solidified and love is kept in working order. When all other rituals fail, take time to remember why you got together in the first place. Go back to the place of your initial connection and restart!

INSIDER'S LOVE TIP
Rituals create a template for endless duplications of romance, but always leave room for a new element to be introduced into familiar surroundings.

Laughter

LOVE

When one part or the other takes itself too seriously, real damage can occur to the relationship. Laughter breaks tension. Playfulness keeps the sparks flying—in a good way.

Many have testified of the healing properties of laughter. The Manufacturer's Manual itself points to this truth: "A cheerful heart is good medicine, but a crushed spirit dries up the bones" (Prov. 17:22 NIV).

Disagreement and tension have short-circuited many a love connection because one part lacked a sense of humor when it was most needed. It is true that not everything in life is funny, but for the most part, upon deeper consideration, most of it is! The ironies of life should furnish many laughs, and folks' foibles should be good for a hoot (as long as no one is being hurt, of course).

When You take yourself too seriously, You tend to see minor irritations and interruptions as much bigger than they are, which makes You cranky and stems the love flow between You and the Man. Sometimes we are too deeply engrossed in ourselves to see and appreciate the mischief of the moment. During those times, reboot to allow your humor program the chance to start fresh.

Get Over Yourself

When You take yourself too seriously, You set yourself up as a god. You declare what is important and what isn't and insist that like You, everyone must eschew humor and embrace the burden of the moment.

Come on! This will never work with the man in your life. It will merely render You a victim of your own insistence and lead only to deeper frustration. Trust me—the moment You insist on being taken seriously, most everyone else will find it a fine time to laugh. Why not join them and celebrate your own silliness? (See Proverbs 15:15.) This approach will lead to better communication and a closer relationship with your partner.

The Ways Humor Helps

It's a Distraction

Humor is disarming. Everyone loves funny people. They get away with murder simply because others are too busy laughing to notice they are being cut. In any comedy club, You see the comedian work his craft, picking on members of the audience who are laughing too hard to mind being insulted.

Case in point: many an argument can be defused through humor. This is not to say that You shouldn't take your partner seriously if he is truly sharing from the heart. But You must know when to engage in the art of distraction if You see him getting too intense about something. Don't let him go to a place of no return.

Using humor to jolt him from his state of anger, frustration, or downright moroseness will bring him back to reality—where, yes, things are sometimes very serious, but they're often not as serious as we make them. He will appreciate your rescue and come to count on it.

It Releases Pressure

Now let's flip the script. Perhaps your partner just laughed at an inappropriate time. Nervous laughter will happen. People laugh when they don't know what to say or how to handle their discomfort. Making them more nervous—by glaring, giving a shove in the ribs, or calling them out in front of others—will not accomplish anything.

Use the moment. Recognize nervous laughter for what it is: a response to tension. Don't criticize your partner (he probably knows he did something inappropriate). Do him a favor by changing the subject to something that is funny so everyone can laugh together. Laughter supplies oxygen to the body, which helps You think more clearly. Once the faux pas has passed, let it go. Always use humor as a friendly device.

It Creates an Amiable Atmosphere

Sometimes a relationship needs extra oxygen—some time to step back, regroup, and come at love from another direction. You should never be in a hurry to make your point. After all, you have a lifetime together and again, much of life is just not that serious unless You make it so.

When the two of you are in conflict about something, creating an atmosphere in which your partner feels threatened does not help You resolve anything. When things get too heated, if possible, find the humor in the moment. Maintain your respect for your partner—help him feel safe—but let playfulness draw you into partnership so you can work through anything.

Wasn't This Supposed to Be Fun?

Remember that the love connection is not simply supposed to function. It should also be fun! Isn't that interesting? The word *fun* is the beginning of the word *function*. Sometimes getting bogged down in the duties of the relationship makes both people forget why they are there in the first place.

You came together because you liked each other. You loved each other. Why? Because you had a great time together and decided you wanted to be with each other for life. You wanted to experience those good feelings and have each other by your sides all the time, so you made the decision to solidify your love.

Now here you are, and all the things that got you together have vanished. A committed relationship is serious, right? The commitment should be serious; however, you shouldn't have heavy-handed exchanges on every single detail of life. The Manufacturer's Manual tells us there is "a time to weep and a time to laugh" (Eccl. 3:4 NIV).

Being able to discern when playfulness is appropriate and having an authentic sense of humor are arts unto themselves, but You can easily master the techniques. Nothing warms the heart like a smile. Nothing is more infectious than laughter. When You can laugh at yourself, the world becomes your oyster. People love to laugh and welcome opportunities to do so!

Humor Killers

If You want to make humor part of your love connection, there are some attitudes and actions to avoid.

Pride

Pride will kill laughter in no time flat. To insist that others take you seriously all the time is really rooted in insecurity and pride—corrosive junk that will clog up the works of your love and damage every important relationship You have if it's not put in check and sent packing.

Pride can lead to foolish (as opposed to playful) behavior. Foolishness can also be just as contagious as laughter. A fool will bring out the fool in You if You try responding in the same way he does. For this reason, it is never good for both partners to yell at the same time. Nothing gets accomplished besides creating noise.

If You let pride make You too serious and insecure, someone in the relationship must shift the mood—change the direction of the interaction—before both crash. Your partner may or may not be equipped to do this. Why risk the relationship? Laughter infuses space and oxygen into the situation and clears the path for a more amenable approach to whatever's happening.

Using Humor Hurtfully

Whatever You do, do not laugh *at* your partner. Laugh *with* him. Laughing at him sets him up to become defensive and shuts down all avenues to a constructive exchange. Laughing *with* your loved one pulls him out of himself and into You, which means You reawaken the desire to solve the problem. He reconnects to the good feelings he wants to experience with You.

This is the power of positive memory: re-creating what was first desirable to lure the other person back to that place. Here, conversation is usually held on an entirely different level, one that will take you both somewhere—hopefully to a wi-fi zone.

INSIDER'S LOVE TIP
Laughter frees You to be your authentic self again, and that is the beginning of every positive connection.

In helping You alleviate stress in your love unit, humor will actually strengthen it, opening all circuits to operate unencumbered by debris. Should You find it stuck from lack of use, simply engage it persistently until its function is restored.

Communication

A h yes, communication. Though one of the most essential components in the love relationship, it is the one the fewest make use of. Small wonder many partners choose to disengage instead of digging in and doing the work to keep their love alive and thriving. The love unit simply cannot function without this application, yet most people don't know how to use it.

You must understand that both parts, You and the Man, will be subject to wear and tear along with an inevitable amount of irritation. After all, you are both imperfect humans. When you fail to use communication, one of the parts will probably stuff, stew, and eventually blow up. This situation can create static (anger and hurt feelings) that disrupts the love flow. What's the point? By the time disruption occurs, the other person has no idea what just happened—or even *why* it happened. At this point, You, the angry partner, list an avalanche of his past sins on top of the current offense. And once You get on a roll . . . well, it's hard to stop. It just feels so good to finally get all of this stuff off your chest. Wow! You can actually breathe again!

Well, what took You so long? You've missed out on breathing freely for far too long. It's a wonder you're still standing. Even though You feel relieved, your partner is dumbstruck. *What was that all about?* he wants to know. The thing is, yelling and exploding do not work. Neither does finger-pointing. That isn't true communication—it's just attacking.

Communication: How to Use It

Notice what the Manufacturer's Manual says: "My dove in the clefts of the rock, in the hiding places on the mountainside, show me your face, let me hear your voice; for your voice is sweet, and your face is lovely" (Song 2:14 NIV).

Yes, there are rules for engaging in positive communication, and this verse states one of them: keep your voice sweet and your face lovely! YOU want him to always look forward to experiencing both. Don't go off on a tear. You'll get much further this way.

Let's look at some other specifics for good communication.

Never Start a Discussion While YOU Are Still Angry (If YOU Can Help It)

When you're angry, YOU might say things you'll later wish YOU hadn't. Words YOU wish YOU could take back are the most harmful to the relationship. So take some time and calm down before YOU decide to deal with the issue.

Never, Ever Confront Your Partner in Front of Others

You're finished before YOU begin if YOU attempt this. Your partner will be so focused on defending himself that he won't hear a word YOU are saying. And he'll resent YOU for humiliating him this way.

Confronting your partner in a crowd involves others in your private business and sets YOU up for major embarrassment. It may damage your reputation. (Who wants to be known as a shrew?) Long after YOU and your partner have moved on and forgotten about the altercation, your observers may not have.

Moral of the story? Keep your business between the responsible parts. That's why it's called a *personal* life.

Take the Time to Assess Why YOU Were Offended

Look at the issue in realistic terms. Is it all about YOU? Take time to discern between real needs and unrealistic desires. Some things are not important enough to make into a major issue and can be handled in a different manner. Confronting your partner when it is not crucial to the love connection turns You into a nag.

And this miserable approach to life gets addictive. The more You complain, the more You will be compelled to complain. If eventually You *do* bring up a problem of true importance, your partner will probably disregard it as trivial—since You get upset over everything. You will have numbed out your partner. The best way to make sure You are really being heard when it matters is by handling the insignificant nits on your own time.

Think about a Solution before You Talk to Him

Never bring up a problem without having a solution in mind. If You just vent your frustration, You will only make your partner feel helpless. Men do not like to feel helpless—it feels like failure—so be constructive in your communication.

Do Not Misjudge Your Partner's Motives

Remember, if he truly loves You, there is a huge chance he didn't know his actions were hurtful, as he would never choose to hurt You on purpose. Therefore, your partner is not the enemy—he's just misguided at the moment. Approaching him in a manner that makes him feel he has to defend himself makes You the enemy and shuts down the lines of communication.

Approach from a Place of Love and Need

After all, You want the relationship to work, right? Do not expect your partner to always know what You see, feel, or need. Cut him some slack, and help him to see your need and feel your pain. Reading minds isn't a common skill. You need to present what is in your heart in a nonthreatening, nonjudgmental, nonaccusatory fashion. This opens the door to his being an empathetic listener.

Set the Atmosphere for Him to Receive What You Have to Say

Focus on his positive points. Positives always put negatives in perspective and minimize them to a workable size. Share what You appreciate about your partner first.

For example: Perhaps he said something that hurt your feelings. Share how You appreciate his ability to always express what he is feeling in an honest fashion. Acknowledge that he may not have realized what he said wounded You.

Now, as we all know, there is usually a morsel of truth in most hurtful statements. Search for it. Find it. Own it. And use it to validate your partner. If he said something critical about your appearance, for instance, acknowledge any truth in his complaint. That being said, also enlighten him as to why and how he can express himself differently in the future to help You get the message without being hurt.

Do Not Beat a Dead Horse
People who tell the truth often have a hard time receiving it, so be gentle. Your partner may feel the need to defend himself. Let him, still keeping in clear view what your objective was at the beginning: reconciliation, not making your point. Forgive him if he asks for it, and move on. This creates a pattern for simple discussions because your beloved knows You are not going to condemn him or retaliate or beat a dead horse to the point of making him fear every conversation with You. He'll see that You want to be close to him, which is a great compliment!

Empower Your Partner
Seal the conversation with a positive statement. For example: "I really appreciate your hearing me. It makes me feel good to know that I can come to you when I'm hurting."

When You Just Need to Talk

These are additional steps to consider if You are not offended but simply need to talk about something.

First, Examine Whether You Have Been Meeting His Needs
If You are not sure, ask. A person who is happy and satisfied will be much more open to fulfilling your requests. You do not want him

to be distracted by all the things you're not doing—he may feel compelled to bring them up—so make sure you've been on your job. Then he can be your advocate.

Be Clear about Why You Need What You Need

If it's really not that important, let it go (You need to pick your battles). If it is critical to your well-being and the well-being of the relationship, be open and well versed on why it is needed and what it will accomplish for both of you.

Clearly Communicate How to Address Your Need

Do not leave this to the guesswork of your partner. This will only create frustration for him. Since the need was not apparent to him in the first place, don't expect him to know what to do about it.

When You go to the doctor and tell him You are in pain, You don't leave him to guess where it is. You show him the exact spot and describe the symptoms. Upon further examination, the doctor writes a prescription. If the prescription is the correct treatment and You take it as directed, You get the healing You desire.

This is true for your relationship as well.

Set a Plan for Improvement

Some things take time, so allow it. Agree to be honest about how You are faring as he makes adjustments. Do not look for immediate change. It took your partner a long time to form the habits he has. As he applies himself to making changes for your sake, be patient and gracious. Speak the truth in love, but give him room to rise to the occasion and become better for You.

Support Him as He Attempts to Meet Your Needs

Let him know when he is getting it right, and help him when he is not. Remember, as You put empowering your partner above your personal need, he will respond by trying to be all that he can be for You.

Do This in Person

One last thing: never, ever send your feelings through e-mail or text messages! Your partner deserves your presence when You are communicating things important to your relationship.

Also, things often don't read as they are written. If he can't hear your voice or see your face while reading how he's not meeting your needs, he may imagine You yelling when perhaps You really aren't. In addition, e-mails don't always get delivered, so You don't want to accuse him of not being responsive when he didn't receive the message in the first place.

Though we live in a technologically progressive society, too much is left to chance when it comes to e-mail. The discussion is worth having face-to-face because there will be less room for misunderstanding.

Agree to Disagree

While attempting to master the fine art of communication, You must always make one final concession. Individuals are just that—individual. Different from each other. Therefore, You must do something uncomfortable from time to time: agree to disagree. You must allow your partner to be who he is. After all, that is the person You fell in love with.

Of course, in any love connection, refinements must occur in both parts. You should enhance and magnify the best in the MAN, and vice versa. But refinements take time and cannot be accelerated. It will take years for your unit to become grounded and mature, but the finished product can be beautiful if You decide to complete the work.

INSIDER'S LOVE TIP
Communication separates those who merely exist side by side from those who thrive and flourish in each other's presence.

That is the exciting part of the operation, if You choose to view it as such. So live and let live. Fix what You can, and leave the rest to GOD.

Honor

To honor someone is to respect, submit to, and praise that person. God says of every person He created: "Those who honor me I will honor, but those who despise me will be disdained" (1 Sam. 2:30 NIV). His creation also craves and needs these habits operating in their lives. These are even more crucial to the life of the love relationship.

Honoring each other gives you both dignity, empowering YOU to love without reserve. This is a universal principle.

> Regardless of culture, gender, and age, everyone seeks validation in the honors he receives from others, this is manifested in different ways within the relationship.

But there are some nonnegotiables when it comes to love that must be present in order for both partners to have a fulfilling connection. YOU must respect the machine if you want it to operate at its best for YOU.

Respect

Aretha Franklin sang about it. She was willing to do anything for her man, but she required respect. Though respect must be earned, it should already be in place if you've reached the point of creating a steady or permanent connection.

Respecting your partner is important because if You don't do it, You will have no desire for him. It's difficult, if not impossible, to feel amorous about someone You don't admire. A lack of respect renders your partner powerless in your mind to operate in any meaningful way in your life.

When a woman operates in a way that tells her Man she does not respect him, that Man will either try to dominate his woman by force or abdicate his role in the relationship altogether.

A Man needs to be needed, and he is wired to take the lead. When he is unable to do so or faces intense criticism, he will feel like a failure. Men are not wired to embrace failure—especially in the eyes and words of their women. They exist to win and wow the significant women in their lives. When this does not happen, they seek other sources of affirmation, which can be another woman, work, sports, some committee or club—anything that makes them feel like a winner.

If a woman does not respect her Man's need to be needed and to lead, the relationship may die altogether. This is a huge reason why women need to *know* they respect any Man they consider for marriage. After forging a permanent commitment, it is too late to try to rearrange someone's entire makeup.

Submit

Submission is another facet of honor. It is the least popular aspect of the love connection. Though the Manufacturer's Manual tells the parts to submit to each other, with the stronger partner giving special care to the externally weaker one, there is still a primary order that must be adhered to in the relationship for it to function the way it was created to (see 1 Pet. 3:1–7).

You must submit to the Man. The Man has been wired to lead, protect, and provide for the woman and cannot accomplish this task if the woman is constantly taking over. But a balance exists that allows You and your partner to counsel together and agree on your strengths and weaknesses. You can decide which of you will be responsible for what. In this way, you maintain cooperation in the relationship and function without offense.

The bottom line is that submission is really teamwork. Every love unit understands the strength and weakness of its parts, and each one is designated to a platform that best supports its function. This works to the advantage of the unit as a whole. Consider sports. In basketball, the guard does not try or want to do what the forward does. In football, the wide receiver does not want to do what the tight end does. If these players step outside of their roles, they'll miss the basket or fumble the ball.

The goal (pardon the pun) should not simply be to have a fabulous romance; it should also be to win at life. To do so, the parts must honor each other's strengths and work in cooperation. In this way, both of you operate at your best, which gains victory for the home team. Yay!

Within the love unit, each part stays in its assigned function, enabling the unit to produce positive output and maintain an optimized operating system over the long haul. Neither part compares its function to the other's. It celebrates its designated program without taking over the other's formats, which would lock up the entire system and even shut down the unit altogether. Each part yields to the other part, allowing it to do what it does best to the benefit of the entire unit.

Submission is not about any part being a doormat. It is not a passive act. It is actively deciding to put yourself in a position to be blessed. It is honoring both the Manufacturer's design for relationships and your partner's ability to lead. To get what You ultimately want—victory in every area of life, from school to home to the workplace—everyone must submit to somebody for the greater good of everyone involved. It's called *order*. Order overrides chaos and injury, bringing peace to everyone.

Praise

Every part could use a healthy dose of praise and appreciation for a job well done. Let me use the sports analogy again. Why are there cheerleaders at a game? Because someone figured out that if a bunch of players heard people cheering them on from the sidelines, they would have the adrenaline rush and strength they needed to win the game.

The same is true in love. It is amazing what praise and appreciation can do. Praise tells your partner You noticed his contribution, which makes him feel good, but it does something deeper, too. It makes him want to be even better for You. Praise and appreciation are addictive. Once You sample a little, You want more—which means You have to come up with something else to do to get them!

Praise cheers your partner on to higher heights and greater acts of love and accomplishment. Even the Manufacturer is quite partial to praise and loves to receive a great review of His handiwork.

Praise is the secret weapon that can get what You want out of your partner when all other tactics fail. Caution: there is a difference between authentic praise and manipulation. Manipulation will be exposed and backfire, and You don't want to go there. Simply find the good parts of your partner and celebrate them. The more You do this, the more good parts he will add.

Let me try another analogy: praise reaps big dividends in your love bank. And every love relationship has one. Regular deposits must be made to ensure that love increases. In order to gain more interest from your partner, You must increase your deposits. These are the positives that heighten his desire to be around You as much as possible because of how You make him feel.

Withdrawals—criticism, repeat offenses, and inconsideration—are like viruses. At least minimize them, but really try to delete them from your interaction altogether. Make sure You check your account periodically to see what state it's in. Never take the balance or the condition of your love unit for granted.

At the end of the day, "I love you," "Thank you," and "I'm sorry; will you forgive me?" are still three of the most powerful phrases in the universe. If You and the MAN use them liberally, you'll see the power they generate—and maintain—in your love unit.

INSIDER'S LOVE TIP
Out of all of the maintenance steps listed, honor is the most powerful. Once this one is mastered, the other steps will actually become easier to perform. Honor has the power to overcome other weaknesses because a good attitude goes a long way in the love unit and fills in the gap for other weaknesses.

5

Accessories

Two are better than one,
because they have a good return for their work:

Increase

If one falls down, his friend can help him up . . .

Support

Also, if two lie down together, they will keep
warm . . .

Intimacy

Though one may be overpowered, two can
defend themselves.

Security

A cord of three strands is not quickly broken.

Longevity

(See Ecclesiastes 4:9-12 NIV)

N ow we get down to the "bling factor"—the fabulous accessories that come with your love package. These parts are not merely for decoration. They are special privileges for those who commit to each other. The Manufacturer has built in these special features to heighten the pleasure of your love connection. If You appreciate them and use them with care, they will add immeasurable power to your love experience. Should You find that a certain accessory does not yet apply to your operating system, file it for later use. Success occurs when opportunity is merged with preparation.

Increase

Let's face it: people want to know what they can get out of everything they do. We all consider this over and over before we take any job, align ourselves with any association, or even decide what vacation we want to go on. *What will I get out of this if I do that?*

Look at what God said to Adam and Eve: "Be fruitful and increase in number, fill the earth and subdue it" (Gen. 1:28 NIV). Therefore, your love connection must produce more than pleasure. The two most important decisions You will ever make are whether You choose to accept Jesus Christ as your Lord and Savior and whom You marry. The former will make the difference in your eternal destination; the latter will affect the quality of life You enjoy while still here on planet earth.

Making the wrong decision in both of these areas will cost You everything. But the right choices will gain You everything—beyond your wildest dreams. The operating system and programs You choose to utilize will affect both how your unit runs and its ability to expand and perform more creative functions.

The Results of a Good Love Connection: Fruit

Luke 6:43 says that "no good tree bears bad fruit" (NIV). So in our relationships, if we develop good connections, we will bear beautiful fruit, both spiritual and natural. Let's take a look.

Spiritual Fruit

Your partner will bring out the worst and the best in You. Let's choose to focus on the best. We're talking love, joy, peace, patience, kindness, goodness, faithfulness, gentleness, and self-control (see Gal. 5:22–23).

These features should be increasing in You on a daily basis because of the MAN's presence. Consider these upgrades to your love file. They will optimize the function and output of your unit.

> The goal is to love your partner more today than yesterday . . . and even more tomorrow.

Love. Love should be increasing. If it is standing still, it has nowhere to go but downhill. Love cannot remain static; it must have movement.

Joy. The joy factor is huge because joy affects your strength. It affects the strength of your love. The strength of your love affects your life: the will to live and love.

Joy is an internal feature that should not be moved or measured by outward stimuli. The primary source of joy is GOD, and it cannot run dry. Other people and things can increase your joy level, but they should never be able to drain the initial supply deposited by God.

You can increase your joy without help from anyone else by increasing your level of service to others and your interaction with the GOD part, since the joy of the Lord will be your strength (see Neh. 8:10). This concept can be looked at in a couple of ways. First, the joy He gives You will give You strength; second, giving him joy will strengthen You. Either way, You end up feeling awfully good! Also, as You pour out to those in need around You and choose to serve your partner, You will become the sole controller of your joy level.

At the end of the day, the joy You possess was not given to You by the world and the world can't take it away. How You handle it, though, will make a world of difference (pun intended) to your personal universe. Many lose their ability to love because they place their joy completely in the hands of their partners. This is a deception. Your beloved will never have enough power to kill your joy, only increase it.

Peace. The strength of your connection—to GOD and to the MAN—should increase your peace. You have two sources of peace at your disposal, and both reassure You that You are not alone. First, God furnishes peace beyond your understanding, empowering You to remain calm even in the midst of hair-raising circumstances. The knowledge that He has the power to override all negative occurrences stabilizes You in the belief that all things ultimately work out to the good for those who are passionately connected to Him (see Rom. 8:28).

Your second source of peace is knowing that all parts of your life are balanced and covered by the connection to your partner. (If You are in the courtship phase, You should have a network of other extensions—family and friends—who fulfill this function in your life until marriage solidifies your connection to the one who will become your first priority.) You share and share alike, which deletes all want from your life. This peace will be interrupted only when you don't walk in agreement.

Pursue peace at all costs (see Ps. 34:14). A major function of the GOD part is reconciliation. Two partners in love continually reconcile as they learn to die daily to secure their oneness.

Patience. The more You know someone, the greater your capacity to exercise patience should become. Knowing his intimate story, along with his needs and fears, supplies information You didn't have before to explain flaws and failures, whether perceived or real. With this type of data in place, You can extend more grace not only to your partner but also to others around You, as You now recognize the signs of their needs as well.

Kindness and goodness. These essentials should increase daily. There are never enough occasions to do something good for your partner, and the more You do, the more You will want to do.

Your delight in serving should become so overwhelming that it spills beyond your relationship to others in need around You. As You accumulate blessings, You should be a blessing to others. Your kindness and goodness become something for others to desire and emulate as these qualities increase in your life.

Faithfulness. This characteristic also should increase in every aspect of your love connection. Faithfulness goes beyond fidelity to the MAN; it extends to acting on your word and keeping your promises to your partner. This involves thinking well of him as well as tangible gestures and kindnesses.

Faithfulness is not just a physical function, it is also a state of mind, a way of existing in and with your loved one. You should see new mercies daily in your relationship because of your faithfulness to each other.

As we saw earlier, faithful are the wounds of a friend if he is waving a sign You need to heed for the sake of the relationship. All signs should point to higher ground and ways to save what might be in danger.

Remaining faithful to honesty in the relationship will preserve it. Faithfulness exerts itself at all costs to provide whatever is needed to redeem the connection. Allow faithfulness to overwhelm You and You will remain faithful.

Gentleness. This quality should increase as You grow in patience, which is required for looking beyond your loved one's faults to his needs. As patience increases, gentleness grows in the way You approach correction and adjustments in the relationship.

The area of touch is also affected. As love grows, so does your gentleness in approaching your partner physically. A reverence undergirds your passion and changes your touch. If you are in the courtship phase, your love will cause you to respect your passion for each other. This respect results in a gentle attitude as you choose to wait for the appropriate time to engage fully.

Gentleness should permeate your spirit. It will be evident in every aspect of your exchange, from how you look at each other to the subtle ways you serve each other. Gentleness gives longevity to the love unit and reduces wear and tear on all parts.

Self-control. Few things protect your relationship like self-control. It keeps both partners focused on what is necessary for the survival and function of their union. Even within the confines of committed love, discipline is required of both parts to protect each of you from injury.

Self-control is not attained just by coming together in marriage. As a matter of fact, your commitment can sometimes ignite appetites and habits that lay dormant before you committed yourselves to each other.

For example: If your partner struggles with lust, marriage will not solve it. Lust may only increase and possibly result in adultery, addiction to pornography, or some other dangerous behavior. Lust—whether it be for sex, alcohol, drugs, shopping, gambling—is like sugar. One taste makes You want more.

Those who struggled with lust before marriage cannot relax simply because they are now connected to a partner for life. Self-control will have to increase because temptation will be greater. As a matter of fact, there will be a whole new set of temptations after You get married—the number of adulterous relationships can testify to that. This is a fact that many are unaware of before marriage. Be on your guard. Many fall because of being uninformed and therefore not equipped to overcome temptation when it presents itself.

> Increase your focus on the outcome You want from your love connection—a great and trustworthy connection that lasts—and then discipline yourself to act accordingly in order to secure it.

Natural Fruit

Children. For married folk, children are usually the first and most obvious area of increase. Adding children to the mix can increase joy, power, and productivity depending on how You nurture them. Your children will imitate the qualities You and the other person produce between you. If they witness love, respect, sound character, and integrity in all you do, they will imitate those things, bringing great pride and blessing to the love your family has as a whole.

Service. For those who have not secured their love connection permanently, increase manifests in a different way. Even people who are courting (i.e., preparing themselves to go to the next level of love) will find numerous opportunities to nurture the lives of those around them. Those who are not married actually have the capacity to nurture more people who need love and maintain more extensions than those who are married (see Isa. 54:1)!

Money. Partnership should bring financial increase. Being attached to another person should empower You to achieve abundance. Please keep in mind that *abundance* means different things to different people. Some define this as lots of material things; others define it as a richness in the intangibles of love, trust, and joy.

Generally speaking, if the woman has not chosen a career as a homemaker, most couples have two incomes to share. If possible, the goal should be to live on one income, then to save and give from the other. Every couple should keep the future (retirement, children, illness) in mind.

Singles should remember that they have the awesome opportunity to clear their debts and build their finances before absorbing anyone else's debts and responsibilities. Programming yourself for financial responsibility now will only contribute to a stronger love connection when You finally engage with someone permanently. You'll be free from virtual debris that could bog down and overload your operating system.

Health and strength. Your partner should not make You sick or sap your strength with ongoing drama. Health and strength are affected by many things—physical ailments, mental stress, pressure, emotional trauma, depression. If you're dating, not married, keep an eye out for this. Sometimes our rose-colored glasses distort the vision we need to see our partners' true qualities and how they may affect us long-term.

Take the time to assess whether You are owning things that You should not be. Absorbing physical, mental, or emotional abuse is not healthy. Get help. Get counseling. Consult the Manufacturer's Manual to rebuild your spirit and override lies with truth for your health's sake. If separation is required for the MAN to take serious steps toward change, handle it wisely. Surround yourself with a support system, and do not suffer alone. Isolation is a deadly virus that has been known to kill many a part and shut down a unit altogether.

Spiritual and intellectual life. Your partner should stimulate You spiritually and intellectually. The old adage is usually true: the couple that prays together stays together. The intimacy that praying together promotes is amazing. (See the Intimacy section of this guide for more details.) And if you share a love for all things intellectual, you will have a much stronger connection.

Remember that increase, both spiritual and natural, is a required function of the love unit. To not grow is certain death. Everything the Manufacturer creates must grow, or it is not fulfilling its original design. Thus, increase is an essential accessory to the love mechanism.

INSIDER'S LOVE TIP
If the MAN is not adding to YOU, he is taking away from YOU. If YOU are not growing, YOU are dying. This is the universal law of generating power, which is exactly what the Manufacturer created the love unit to do.

Support

Life is a marathon—no, a relay race. It is impossible to run the entire distance alone. As I stated previously, the Manufacturer has wired every part for reliance on other parts, which is why teamwork enables You and the Man to function at optimum levels.

Both of you need to know that someone has your back, that someone is there to take over when you run out of steam.

> For a relationship to be successful, a support program must be securely in place.

This software empowers both partners to serve as backup for each other, while also optimizing both systems.

The program stabilizes the couple when they are feeling shaky, doubtful, or weary, and it also compels both partners to venture out of their comfort zones, to grow, and to climb to higher heights.

Encouragement

Both partners do their best work by first encouraging each other. This truth is in keeping with what the Manufacturer's Manual says: "Let us consider how we may spur one another on toward love and good deeds" (Heb. 10:24 NIV).

There are three main aspects of encouragement.

1. Listening
Everyone appreciates being heard. Listening to your partner's heart and dreams shows that what he has to offer is worthy of an audience. This validation gives your loved one the courage to pursue what he's been thinking about.

2. Serving
After You hear what the other person has shared, make yourself available to serve in whatever way he needs You to reinforce his power and encourage him to move forward. Your encouragement helps the MAN to formulate a plan and carry it out. This is evidence of true teamwork (or cooperation of parts in a love unit).

3. Praying
Praying for your partner will accomplish what your words and physical availability cannot. In the midst of prayer, not only will You gain insight into how You can be a more effective helper, but You will also enlist heaven to help your partner. This is powerful! Your prayers will enable your partner to receive the instruction he needs to perform his function and the power to do it well.

All prayers connect to the Manufacturer, who then distributes power to the one You prayed for where and when he needs it. Praying together empowers both of you, as there is always maximum power in agreement.

Maximum Strength

Strong love units regularly run diagnostics to assess the strengths and weaknesses of their parts. This is done not to condemn or belittle the members of the unit but to determine the best functions for each part.

Again, this is not a finger-pointing exercise but a strategic meeting of the MIND parts in order to form the strongest relationship that will effectively preserve the life of your love.

What makes a good unit a great unit—the type that creates fabulous output—is the ability to accommodate and perform each other's functions should there be a need to do so. After agreeing on your roles (who does what in the relationship), each partner always stands ready to fill in for the other one if it becomes necessary. This is called exchanging strength for strength.

As long as the parts are able to back each other up, the entire unit runs smoothly and accomplishes exactly what it was designed to do: produce excellent data and results. No unit is concerned with which part was more excellent; only the bottom line output and the longevity of its performance count.

Finally, You must be a support to the one supporting You. Some partners make it difficult to be supportive. Allow yourself to be encouraged and helped, and lend your support at the appropriate time. It is the relay effort within the relationship that keeps you both strong enough to function at your greatest strength.

Without this support in place, both of you would eventually implode. Support is vital to the life of a relationship, whether it be technical, hands-on support; spiritual support, as in your partner's praying for You when all physical efforts have been exhausted; or quiet and gentle support, soundlessly letting your partner know that you're there and You have his back. In whatever form it appears, support pours into and strengthens the love connection, making it a force to be reckoned with.

INSIDER'S LOVE TIP
Without this program running in the unit, neither part can be anchored. Free-floating parts do not form a solid unit and can fall prey to outside sources, predisposing them to fail in maintaining their connection.

Intimacy

This is most people's favorite part of a relationship. The Manufacturer's Manual records one woman as saying, "Let him kiss me with the kisses of his mouth—for [his] love is more delightful than wine" (Song 1:2 NIV).

Everyone looks forward to intimacy, the physical and emotional expression of passion, the desire two partners have for each other. Unfortunately, this program is misused as much as it is enjoyed. As I mentioned earlier, because of the power associated with this particular accessory, physical intimacy should not be introduced to the love unit prematurely. It is appropriate only after a permanent link has been established.

The Problem with Too Much, Too Soon

To install this accessory early in the relationship has lasting implications. Let's look at a few of them.

Intimacy Scrambles Trust

Premature physical intimacy creates a less-than-stable platform for the rest of the relationship to function on. It also can be deceptive, causing both partners to believe they've found the right person when in fact chemistry has clouded their capacity to discern the long-term effects of their association. Generally, after some time passes, both people come to realize they are not really compatible at all, leading them to sever the relationship.

Relationship Residue

Ending the relationship can be extremely painful because intricate signals crossed when they were imitating oneness. Upon severing ties, these signals are damaged irreparably as what must be stripped away cannot be replaced. Each person is still imprinted, however faintly, on the other's spirit. These imprints can never be erased.

Sexual intimacy was designed as a glue to bind a couple together permanently after marriage. Therefore, I strongly advise You not to install this accessory prior to marriage. If You have done so, submit your body back to the Lord. Ask for his forgiveness, forgive yourself, and purpose to move forward in a manner that honors God as well as yourself (see 1 Cor. 6:18–20).

Sexual Intimacy Has Tremendous Power

Many parts make the mistake of centering their connection around this particular accessory. Notice that intimacy is called an *accessory* and not an *essential part*, though in a lot of ways it is a very necessary part. Intimacy is a gift from the Manufacturer to You and the Man to sweeten the love connection, but it can rule the connection or detract from its power if handled improperly.

Married couples: though the Manufacturer urges that You not withhold this function from your partner except for times of prayer and fasting, the love unit cannot rely on this function alone to power the entire connection.

Sexual intimacy is especially powerful because it can render one part a slave to the other. It is in essence the natural parallel to the spiritual act of worship. As stated before, one of the words for *worship* in Greek—*proskuneo*—literally means to "kiss forward" or "kiss God." As we press into God, an intimate connection is made and an exchange of power occurs. We surrender our power to God and

He implants His Spirit within us, creating life—the type of life that empowers us to become more like GOD.

We exchange something with GOD we cannot exchange with anyone else. This is what builds intimacy between us. The same is true for YOU and the MAN. This most personal of exchanges emotionally and spiritually builds intimacy between the two of you that culminates with a physical merge. This accessory should be respected and used with care.

Physical "Worship"

If we look at intimacy in terms of the Manufacturer's Manual, we can say that a woman is like the Holy of Holies and a MAN is like the high priest. Back in the day, when the high priest went into the Holy of Holies to minister, the glory of God would come down and consume the offering the priest laid before Him (see 2 Chron. 7:1; Lev. 9:23–24).

In much the same way, as a MAN and a woman minister to each other physically, both are consumed by each other. In this act, we essentially model that glorious experience of finally becoming one with GOD at the end of the age. The feeling of ecstasy experienced in the marriage bed is a foretaste of what we will experience eternally.

Indeed, we will have to be refitted with glorified bodies because earthly vessels will not be able to contain such a powerful feeling without exploding! This type of "worship" practiced by married partners is another form of "having church" or "communion" in the privacy of your own "sanctuary"—your bedroom. God leaves the regularity of enjoying this gift to YOU and your partner's discretion.

"Knowing" Each Other

In review, it is important to clarify that both worship and sex involve giving all YOU are and all YOU have to the one YOU love. Sexual intimacy promotes one person's "knowing" the other person on a deeper level. What can result is conception (physical and spiritual), which gives birth to new life in the connection.

Earlier we read in the first section of the Manufacturer's Manual (the book of Genesis), Adam "knew" Eve (see the King James translation), and she conceived. This is the pattern of regeneration within the love relationship.

"Knowing" equals intimacy. When we "know" GOD, we conceive the fruit of the Spirit and bear the attributes of Christ to the world. The connection promotes change, overriding anything that does not reflect the nature of GOD in us.

The same is true between the couple in a love relationship. Sexual intimacy is binding. It becomes the place where two souls search for each other and take hold, sharing and exchanging secrets. Two hearts are bound together by the unspoken things they share.

This can be beautiful or dangerous, depending on the participants. It will always be unsafe to make yourself this vulnerable to a person who has not committed his life to YOU. To do so is to open your HEART to lasting damage from overexposure to elements that are hostile to your personal security. Generally speaking, it is the woman who sustains the most damage in most of these scenarios.

Premature sexual intimacy can render a woman completely powerless. She becomes a slave of sorts, in some cases physically but in most cases emotionally and spiritually. It becomes hard to sever the connection after sexual intimacy. If the MAN chooses to move on after having enjoyed her giving her all to him, he leaves her to suffer from damaged self-esteem and rejection, seeking parts of herself she can never get back.

The other danger is that premature intimacy opens YOU up to life-altering consequences, such as life-threatening viruses, that can affect your health and even kill YOU. The only way to minimize these dangers is to follow the rules set out in the Manufacturer's Manual (see Prov. 8:33–36). Again, do not attempt to assemble or add intimacy to your connection until YOU have been permanently linked to your partner for life.

Another Brand of Intimacy

Before You and the Man form the permanent link, you can utilize an even more powerful intimacy program that will work as a great complement to sex after making your lasting commitment. This form of intimacy is that of transparency: open communication, where Minds and Hearts meet and exchange information vital to each other.

Transparency actually feeds passion, the passion needed for sexual intimacy. Mental and spiritual intimacy set the stage for commitment by establishing faithfulness between you. This is a prerequisite to establishing a permanent bond.

The secret to having a powerful and satisfying exchange begins with prayer. I've mentioned that prayer is an intimacy builder, one that solidifies the connection between two partners with a bond that can be felt. It empowers a couple to withstand outside pressure that could threaten the security of their love connection.

Restart all programs with prayer daily to keep the connection sound and running at its greatest capacity (see 1 Thes. 5:17; Luke 18:1–8).

What Makes Intimacy Work

> Communication is the secret to intimacy in and out of the marriage bed.

You will need to know how to communicate well to enhance the sexual experience. A guided tour of your body, as well as some discussion about what You like and don't like, will help your partner serve You in a fulfilling and pleasurable manner.

Do not leave anything to chance. Many couples merely tolerate each other in the marriage bed because they don't have the courage to communicate their physical needs to each other. In the interest of not hurting feelings, some partners settle for being unsatisfied. On some level, this dissatisfaction manifests elsewhere in the relationship in negative ways. To experience and maintain pleasure and satisfaction, both partners must be willing to communicate.

The key to making intimacy work is to not take yourself too seriously. Approach physical intimacy as a fun way to discover how you can give each other surges of power.

Again, because this is a form of worship, transparency is critical to its being a pleasurable experience.

Healthy Guidelines for Intimacy

Because this particular accessory can be habit-forming and even addictive, it is important to maintain healthy guidelines for the preservation of the love unit.

Never Do Things That Offend the Other Person

Discuss what gives you both pleasure, and honor what makes your partner uncomfortable. Good lovers are not selfish. They are focused on pleasing their beloved and derive their enjoyment from making sure the other person is satisfied first (see Philippians 2:3).

Don't Expect Intimacy to Create Love

Intimacy is a response to love rather than a generator of it. Thus, the phrase "making love" is an inaccurate one. You cannot make what does not already exist. Nurture, yes; create, no. Always give respect, consideration, and appreciation in intimacy, and it will increase your pleasure.

Prepare for Intimacy

Intimacy must start at the beginning of the day and build to a crescendo by the time a couple comes together. Trying to jump-start intimacy before both parts are ready can prove disappointing, if not disastrous. Plan for intimacy, and take the steps to cultivate it for the ultimate in satisfying experiences.

INSIDER'S LOVE TIP
Intimacy can make a temporary connection permanent. Flirtation and romance, however, must remain a part of the program to keep your love functioning at full capacity.

The power of engagement via physical intimacy is often underestimated or used in an improper context. Celebrating this accessory regularly will empower the two main parts—that would be You and your Man—to contribute greater output that will serve to optimize your love systems.

Security

N o love connection can survive unless both parts feel safe. There is no way around it. Knowing that someone has your back, that You are loved in spite of how You look when You wake up in the morning or even if You just made a major fool of yourself, is unspeakably satisfying. Knowing the MAN looks at You and says, "I love You anyway" makes You feel safe.

Certainly security is what the Manufacturer offers us in His Manual: "The Lord replied, 'My Presence will go with you, and I will give you rest'" (Exod. 33:14 NIV). "I will never leave you or forsake you" (Josh. 1:5).

Years ago, there was a famous song called "You and Me against the World." That phrase sums up the kind of security a good relationship provides. Knowing that You are not alone in your struggles, that there is an oasis where You can rest your weary mind and burdened heart, is a huge relief—and an essential component to the love connection.

What to Protect

Let's look at the things You value and want to know are safe.

Your HEART
You want to know that You are not sleeping with the enemy, so to speak. You want to feel secure enough to share your fears, dreams, questions, and all the things that are authentically You without being criticized,

demeaned, or rejected. This is huge for You, but it is also huge for the MAN, especially if he's been taught to be distrustful of women.

Both of you should feel safe enough to express yourselves without thinking twice about the other's reaction. As a matter of fact, You should think that if anyone on the planet understands You, it's your partner. You should enjoy feeling the freedom to expose the most vulnerable parts of yourself—emotionally and spiritually if You are dating, physically as well as emotionally and spiritually if You are married.

Your MIND and Emotions

Your MIND and your emotions must be safe with your partner. The thoughts he feeds You and the way he makes You feel are essential to your well-being. The rest of the world screams loudly, questioning your worth and everything about You. The one You love should be your safe place where your worth is settled and confirmed.

You are valuable. You matter to someone, and his presence in your life adds a greater degree of definition to all that You already are. Who You are has already been established by God, and now the MAN adds another dimension that becomes a plus only if all systems are right for connection. As Adam named Eve, giving her definition as the "mother of all living things," your beloved names You according to your purpose in his life. The way your partner responds to You shapes your own assessment of your worth and who You are.

If You are with a part who abuses his power in the relationship, You can find yourself broken and feeling threatened. But a positive love connection will bear the fruit of making You and the MAN even more secure in who You are and what You have to offer others.

Your Physical Being

The other safety concern is physical. Just knowing your loved one is near should put your mind at ease and alleviate the angst of being alone. You will find, after spending time aligning yourself with another person, how quickly You become used to his presence and miss it when he isn't around.

The rest that comes from having someone to lean on, pull You up, hold You close when You need reassurance is something too wonderful to describe. In the arms of your partner, You find a physical as well as emotional and spiritual safe haven.

Why is safety so important? Every single person has felt vulnerable at one time or another. Some try to take advantage of single people because they have no one to defend or protect them physically, fiscally, or emotionally.

Knowing that You don't have to deal with any situation alone is a great source of comfort and a gift. In some instances, familiarity will breed contempt. This is something every couple should guard against, choosing instead to celebrate their closeness and all it represents in the forms of security and peace.

How the GOD Part Helps

Knowing that someone else is in your life to help You shoulder the weight of the world is overwhelmingly reassuring. Still, every person needs the Power Source as his or her primary supply of comfort and strength.

In the midst of your relationship, GOD remains a constant fixture, empowering both partners to live their best lives and give their best to each other. And when all other supports fail, GOD reminds You of His presence and the power He brings to grant restoration and healing to the broken and weary.

In returning to the GOD part and dwelling in the assurance that His power is all You need, You will find your strength coming back. It is wise to make the GOD part your primary source of security before adding other sources to the mix. Life is subject to shift, causing upheavals from time to time that You or your partner will have no control over. In these moments, it is important not to cast away your confidence in the GOD part because it will keep You and the MAN intact, restoring divine order to all systems operating the love unit.

Security is critical to the grounding process of every love unit. It must be in place to ensure the strength and duration of the connection between You and the Man. Without it, the love unit will be unstable at best with a propensity for shorts and, ultimately, disengagement. One should check regularly for breaks or cracks and repair immediately.

INSIDER'S LOVE TIP
Security and confidence give us the boldness to approach all situations in life knowing that they are solvable. Resting in the knowledge that help is always available—from the God piece if not from each other—removes all fear and allows both parts to see the victory ahead of its manifestation.

Longevity

The greatest preserver of life is the overall feeling of well-being—being at peace with God, yourself, and the other people in your world. When it comes to the love connection, the love You feel must be reinforced by something other than the MAN for you as a unit to experience longevity. (As You can see, longevity is closely tied to Security.)

Relationally and spiritually, the answer to longevity is the same: at the end of the day, it is the GOD part that will keep You and the MAN joined together in a solid bond that cannot be easily broken. It is this connection that will renew your relationship and alleviate the effects of time, wear, and tear that threaten the life of the love You share emotionally, physically, and spiritually.

The reality is that anyone can commit to a steady dating relationship or marriage. *Staying* together is the difficult thing to master. You cannot truly say your relationship is a success until it has weathered the test of time. This is the lasting testimony that love conquers all.

Love Must Succeed

Because true love is always growing, longevity cannot be installed in the love unit until it has endured a series of tests. Remember that the Manufacturer designed love to go the distance and endure the test of time; therefore, it is possible.

The knowledge that You and your partner are both accountable to a source greater than yourselves should ensure the life and quality of your relationship. As You approach your relationship with reverence, purposing to make it a nurturing and healthy place to be as well as something that honors GOD, GOD will always furnish You with everything You need to keep your love connection powerfully engaged.

INSIDER'S LOVE TIP
Longevity is something others will want after seeing yours. Determine to be an example to others.

Longevity is an accessory that is becoming harder and harder to find, so it is expensive. It will cost You something to obtain it, but the price will be well worth it.

6

Troubleshooting

"Call upon me, and I will answer [you]; I will be with [you] in trouble, I will deliver. . . ."

—PSALM 91:15 NIV

If your unit has no power . . .

There might be a compatibility issue. Check out You and the Man for common interests. Opposites may attract, but they are usually unable to sustain a lasting connection.

Two of the top sources of dissention between couples are sex and money. Have thorough discussions on these topics before engaging. Refer to the Assembly portion of this guide to review the other areas that must be inspected before attempting to form a permanent connection.

Be willing to admit that the person You are trying to connect to may have all the right outward features but not be a good match for You internally. This has no bearing on your quality. Neither does it affect your desirability. You simply must wait for and be able to recognize the right match to achieve an effective exchange.

The Manufacturer's Manual says, "Do not plow with an ox and a donkey yoked together" (Deut. 22:10 NIV). If it doesn't fit, don't force it. You will never be able to fix the other person. Consider whether You can live with your potential partner as is. If not, move on. There is no shame in that.

Most men know early on what type of connection they want to have with You. Invest your time wisely, only in connections that are intentionally moving forward to a permanent love connection. In most cases, a year is enough to determine whether this is a positive association.

Again, do not ignore the red flags. They will grow larger and wave more frantically after you've "sealed the deal." Keep in mind that

Note: Remember, it's not how you *look* together but how you *function* together that counts.

You are seeking a long-term connection, not temporary gratification. Check your potential partner out thoroughly, and deal realistically with your findings. Keep in mind that this MAN is not the only MAN in the universe. If all the necessary elements aren't lining up, keep shopping!

If there's static in the
connection . . .

To remove static from the connection, You will need to clear the lines of communication. That requires removing You and your opinion from your exchange so that You can clearly hear what your partner is saying. If your goal as a couple is to seek peace and pursue reconciliation, you can neither stand stubbornly on principle nor focus on defending yourself in the midst of your dialogue.

Listening first and seeking how You can serve your partner will create a powerful bond and end up serving You in the end. To get what You want, You sometimes have to give it first. The Manufacturer's Manual reminds us, "Do nothing out of selfish ambition or vain conceit, but in humility consider others better than yourselves" (Phil. 2:3 NIV).

Learning to talk offensively versus defensively in your relationships leaves the door open for honest and constructive dialogue that eventually results in the outcome You are after. Remove pride and your so-called rights from the exchange, and focus on empowering your partner to make the right choice for both of you.

Try asking questions instead of just arguing your point. This action releases your partner to consider your point of view and empowers him to make a good decision. He can be a champion for your cause as well as a vital part of the team that makes your love connection work.

Note: Make better communication a priority and You will produce the results You truly want: sustained electricity and optimized love.

Because your partner feels that You sincerely seek to be a blessing to him, he will want to bless You back. This mutual desire removes all resistance to moving forward as a strong couple.

If the battery is dead . . .

Weariness from routine is death to the power of a couple. To jump-start your relationship, you will need to revisit why the two of you chose to be connected in the first place. Rekindling romance is crucial to recharging your love battery.

Remember Jesus' words in the Manufacturer's Manual: "You have persevered and have endured hardships. . . . Yet I hold this against you: You have forsaken your first love" (Rev. 2:3–4 NIV).

Forming a permanent link is only one step in the life of a relationship. Romance must continue. The desire to solve conflicts must continue. The constant search for what will please the other person must continue. Never take the other part for granted—the moment You do, You are in danger of being either filed away or deleted and replaced.

Remain present and alert in your relationship. Do not ignore any cues such as power waning or signals flashing in your partner's eyes. Reconnect and recharge. Do not allow large amounts of time to pass before You reconnect.

Remember, romance does not just happen—You have to plan for it. So set the mood. Make a date. Do whatever You have to do to put the spark back in your relationship. When in doubt, ask your partner what is missing. Do not be offended by the answer. Receive the information, and use it to the benefit of the relationship.

If the need arises, repent, say You are sorry for allowing things to degenerate to where they are now, and covenant with your partner to start afresh.

Remember how You started out, and revisit that place. Do the things You did before and add a new twist to them. Learn to laugh and celebrate your love. Jump-start your new beginning today!

Note: Batteries need to be recharged on a regular basis in order to maintain power. Keep your charger handy.

If parts are defective . . .

Please note that no part is perfect—with the exception of the GOD piece. People, and even your own personal parts, will fail YOU. This is the law of wear and tear over time. That said, when You conclude that the MAN has a defect, You must determine whether the defect damages the quality of the love connection or just irritates You.

Things that fall under the serious, love-threatening category are adultery, addictions, abuse, and irresponsibility that affects the physical safety and security of the family unit. Failure to pick up one's socks, habitual lateness, laziness, or any other things that irritate but do not endanger must be put in the right perspective and dealt with. For the latter, the Manufacturer's Manual reminds us, "We who are strong ought to bear with the failings of the weak" (Rom. 15:1 NIV).

Also, in cases of the latter, remember that when You point a finger, your partner can and will likely respond with: (1) You chose him to be in your life; (2) You knew about these issues earlier in the relationship and still chose to connect to the MAN; (3) You do things that irritate him just as much as he irritates You! (He just hasn't said anything, or perhaps he has in subtle ways You haven't noticed.)

Love-threatening defects should be prayerfully considered. Seek counsel, and then do what You have to do to preserve your life and state of well-being. Do not remain in life-threatening situations. GOD generates only life and has nothing to do with death. He considers all those He created to be precious.

Find a support system to help You remove yourself. In some instances, until your partner experiences loss as a consequence to his actions, he will see no need to change. Choose actions over lip service to make a statement. Then stick to your convictions and do not reconnect unless your partner has made drastic and consistent changes.

Be accountable to someone outside of the relationship who can offer unbiased and wise counsel. Then allow yourself the time to heal so You can make clear decisions that aren't based on fear or desperation.

Note: Nagging never works. It only ingrains the defect deeper in your MIND as well as in the actions of your partner. Choose to focus on the positive output, and the negative will be diminished, if not totally removed.

For all the minor and major irritations, choose to love anyway. Instead of demanding change from him, seek to find how You can serve your partner and inspire him. Focusing on what You love about him will help You overlook faults more easily.

Finally, always pursuing peace and building up your partner will make him want to be his best for You.

If parts are unresponsive . . .

One must look underneath the surface of an unresponsive partner to find the source of the problem. Though each case is
unique, there are several reasons for this difficulty.

First, generally speaking, people are the accumulation of their life
experiences. They come to relationships preprogrammed from all
their former love connections. They observed how to love from their
parents, who may or may not have been a good illustration of what
love looks like. And they've learned about it from how they've been
treated in past relationships.

A person may be unresponsive emotionally and/or sexually. (Obviously, the latter applies only to those who have made a permanent
connection.) If your partner is emotionally cold, you'll experience
problems in communication and affection. You will need to practice
patience and loving consistency while giving God (He is the only
one who can change someone—and that someone must be willing)
the time and room needed to transform the unresponsive person into
a sharing and affectionate partner.

Because many males struggle with expressing emotion, it will take
time, insight, and patience on your part to draw your partner out and
locate the problem. Setting the atmosphere for him to feel safe will
be up to You. Appreciation and praise will compel him to give more
of himself over time.

In some instances, depending on how reserved your partner is, You
may have to shift your focus to the things he does that show You he

cares and accept him as he is. Usually, this tactic is the most effective at transformation. Should his emotional numbness continue long-term, however, with no change or signs of willingness to change, You may have to consider how damaging it is to You. If You are still in the courtship stage, remember that what You see is what You will get, so decide whether You want to live with his present program for the rest of your life. Don't bank on his changing because he may not. If you're married, You are in covenant, which means "'til death do us part." Unless his behavior is life-threatening, You will need to exercise all options to reach a workable solution for your connection.

For those of you who have formed a permanent love connection, per-haps You started off with a physically responsive, affectionate, commu-nicative, vibrant partner, and you've noticed a change—a withdrawal. This will require deeper investigation. The first and most common fac-tor is stress. Stress can render anyone unable to function—yes, even sexually. If desire is present but the ability to function is not, physical problems could also be a factor, so he should consult a physician.

Offense and unresolved anger can also be a major factor in unre-sponsiveness. Bitterness can seriously hinder desire. Take the time to make sure You don't have any outstanding issues with your partner that have caused him to shut down on You. Be willing to ask for forgiveness in order to resolve this problem.

Pay attention to his friends as well as to any changes in his pattern of behavior. If You cannot account for large blocks of his time or You find he has become vague about his whereabouts and actions, beware. This situation can be painful but it is one You must face because it can put your life in danger: if your partner is having relations with people outside your connection, he could expose you to sexually transmitted diseases. This, of course, could be the least likely reason for your MAN's withdrawal, but You should consider it if the signs are there.

Do not ignore changes that make You uncomfortable. Do not be afraid to ask your partner questions.

Avoid the urge to ditch an unresponsive partner. Take the time to diagnose the problem before coming to a decision on how You will move forward. Keep in mind that the goal should always be to seek reconciliation and reestablish peace. The Manufacturer's Manual says, "You must protect me from the foxes, foxes on the prowl, foxes who would like nothing better than to get into our flowering garden" (Song 2:15 MSG).

Recognize that your partner is not the enemy in your struggle to be together. The forces of destruction are against your connection; face them together.

> **N**ote: There is a price to be paid for every love connection that is abandoned. Therefore, make love your goal. It can cover a multitude of sins and restore even the most broken of parts.

If fuses are blown . . .

It is impossible not to get angry. Even God gets angry. How we channel anger is the issue. The Manufacturer's Manual reminds us to "be quick to listen, slow to speak and slow to become angry" (James 1:19 NIV). God also urges us to "be angry and do not sin," along with His suggestion, "Do not let the sun go down on your wrath" (Eph. 4:26 NKJV). In other words, resolve that mess before YOU go to bed! Allowing issues to escalate to the point of explosion will be detrimental to the relationship and will most assuredly corrupt the bond between parts.

It is important to take steps that promote calm and effective communication. If YOU are shouting, YOU are only exacerbating the problem. The other person can't hear YOU because his natural reaction is to defend himself against any type of onslaught. In the end, nothing gets resolved, and the possibility of deeper offense remains in the wake of a blowout.

Taking the time to really listen to your partner, whether YOU agree or not, will actually empower YOU to find a solution. What he is sharing will be full of invaluable clues to the actual problem. By taking the time to ask questions, YOU can find clarity on what it will take to find a working solution you can both live with. Remember to approach all difficulty in the spirit of reconciliation—not "winning."

Watch your words. Most partners speak first and think later, but it is far better to flip the script. Consider what YOU want to achieve. Is what YOU are going to say helpful to accomplishing your goal?

Discard the words that could be inflammatory, and choose words that will be healing instead.

Begin to master your emotions. They do follow your lead. If You really believe in your heart of hearts that your partner is not out to get You, You will react to him in a different manner.

Anger is actually a response to unyielded rights. So throw out the rules and expectations You have of others. They might not even be aware of these "codes of conduct"! Remember that, for the most part, if people "knew better, they would do better." In this context, anger is the last emotion that is appropriate.

Note: The opposite of anger is calm. Purpose to calmly assess the situation before reacting, and allow peace to prevail over all your responses and decisions.

If you need to salvage a
broken part . . .

P eople, parts, and connections get broken. Sometimes, people just leave. If the MAN disconnects permanently, you'll need to choose your reaction. Holding on to the offense and submerging yourself in bitterness makes YOU a slave to sin, and to him, which will ultimately kill your ability to function in love.

Rather, whenever offense occurs, YOU must own your part and release the rest. Your reaction is the only aspect of the disconnection YOU can do something about. The offenses that others commit against YOU only highlight their weaknesses—as well as the areas that are still open and vulnerable inside of YOU. In every offense is a grain of truth about YOU or the other person that needs to be exposed and dealt with.

Hurtful words, shocking betrayals, rejection—all these things can truly devastate the heart and leave YOU wondering if life can continue after such great pain. If all things truly work to the good of those who love God (see Rom. 8:28), YOU must trust Him in times when your love is blindsided that the ugly can be redeemed and transformed into something beautiful. If YOU choose to release your pain and refuse to either carry or harbor it, YOU are on your way to transformation.

When YOU harbor offense, YOU give the MAN waaay too much power over YOU. If you've abdicated your power, YOU lack what YOU need to cooperate with GOD in securing your healing and recovery from your situation. The truth YOU must receive in the midst of all the pain is that GOD is still in His place. YOU are still loved. YOU are not alone. And the greatest truth is that He can repair HEARTS, no matter how broken or shattered. YOU can recover from this and be even greater than before.

This is the law of refurbishment. More attention gets paid to the broken pieces than to those supposedly in mint condition. Those that are reinforced and restored stand stronger than those that never sustained an injury.

But the choice is yours. Will YOU receive the restoration available to YOU? See the Tech Support portion of this guide, and follow the directions. In the meantime, decide willfully to forgive. The Manual instructs us, "Bear with each other and forgive whatever grievances you may have against each other. Forgive as the Lord forgave you" (Col. 3:13 NIV).

When necessary, open your hands and let your partner go. Remember: nothing new can be put into closed hands.

> **N**ote: No person is worth abdicating the beauty of who YOU are. This is one thing he is unable to take from YOU.

If you want to avoid negative
buildup . . .

If You reboot your love unit on a regular basis, You will avoid having to endure a major overhaul down the line. A clean machine will always run smoother than one that accumulates negative buildup and overloaded operations.

Occasionally, run a diagnostic scan of your machine. Ask your partner, "How am I doing? Where do we want to go from here? How can we move forward in a way that increases our love?" The excitement of adding power to your love should energize both of you.

Your relationship with your significant other deserves time and attention because it affects your well-being and has a lasting impact on every area of your life. Pay attention to the little things, and feel free to openly discuss areas of concern before they turn into cataclysmic corrosives.

It is no one's fault but your own if You are suffering in silence in your relationship. Though You are serving your partner, love should be an empowering experience. If You are being drained and depleted, You are either doing too much or accepting too much responsibility for the relationship. Choose to be a victor and not a victim. Love is not slavery; it is an opportunity to serve, making You and the one You serve better.

Examine how You are acting and why. Get rid of actions not conducive to wholeness and healing and power. Do not rob your partner of being able to serve and grow by taking on his work as well as your own in the relationship. This will only get You left in the long run, and you'll be bitter about it.

Set relationship boundaries that protect your HEART, your health, and your joy. Openly discuss these things with your partner so that you walk in agreement. Don't be ashamed to ask for assistance when You need it and to offer assistance when You see that it is needed.

Avoid negative buildup by doing regular virus scans and defragmenting to keep your connections clear. If something is bothering You, talk about it when You can do so calmly. You will be surprised to find that after You have a heart-to-heart with the one You love, the problem seemed much larger than it really was.

Note: A hands-on approach to love will always be effective. This is the one area in which micromanaging can yield great returns!

Throw out negative records and record positive occurrences. Rehearse and vocalize the good things often, remembering to express appreciation. Reward your partner for good behavior with things he enjoys. And then do something to earn your own reward.

Recalibration can be fun as well as hard work. Incorporate both into your love unit and watch its power increase.

QUICK REFERENCE GUIDE

1. Plan for love—it doesn't just happen. As with every other area of life You plan for, being open and expectant will prepare your HEART for the inevitable—it will happen when You are ready.
2. Make room for love—it won't force its way into your midst. It needs to be a priority. It will not submit to your terms.
3. Make sure You install a "we" program—love is not just about You. It's about your partner, too. Don't make him feel left out.
4. Remember that your primary goal is to serve your partner. As You make someone else's life better, You will reap the rewards.
5. Get rid of rules that hinder You from having a great love experience. Install humor and flexibility into your relationship.
6. Choose your battles wisely—prefer relationship to principle.
7. Remain your authentic self—and allow your partner to do the same.
8. Communicate, communicate, communicate! Remember that each of you has needs and history the other one doesn't know about.
9. Decide to always believe the best about your partner.
10. Decide that once a permanent connection has been made, disconnection is not an option. Determine to do whatever it takes to make your love go the distance.
11. Whatever You do—never disconnect from the GOD piece.

CUSTOMER SERVICE

In the relationship, You are your own customer service department. Customer service begins with You. Consider your partner your best customer. Look at the Manufacturer's Manual: "For even the Son of Man [Jesus] did not come to be served, but to serve, and to give his life as a ransom for many" (Mark 10:45 NIV). I've said already that as You seek to serve your partner, You will find that You also get served. A happy customer will reciprocate.

In the giving, You receive more than what You give. Above and beyond reciprocation, You receive the fulfillment of knowing that You contributed to and made a difference in the life of someone else. This is what parts and connections do at optimum function: they create lives that matter.

TECH SUPPORT

"But the Counselor, the Holy Spirit . . . will teach you all things and will remind you of everything [Christ has] said to you."
—JOHN 14:26 NIV

- For help on any love issue, dial 1-800-12-JESUS.
- The operator will put You right through.
- There will be no computer prompts. Your call will not be put on hold.
- Your questions will be answered in a timely and effective manner.
- For quality assurance purposes, your call will be recorded in heaven.
- If further assistance is needed, a ministering angel along with earthly counsel will be dispatched to You immediately.

After receiving instruction, please refer to the Manufacturer's Manual and follow the directions listed there to ensure quality service to all parts involved.

WARRANTY INFORMATION

"Love never fails."
—1 Cor. 13:8 NIV

PLEASE NOTE THAT IF YOU ARE A CONSUMER ON ANY CONTINENT IN THE WORLD, THIS WARRANTY HAS NO TERRITORIAL RESTRICTIONS OR EXPIRATION. (In other words, it's honored everywhere!)

PARTS: Heaven, Inc., warrants to the original user that God-branded products will be free from defects in workmanship under normal, God-ordained usage for as long as the parts have life, as they are fearfully and wonderfully made.

EXCLUSIONS: This warranty excludes (1) Any parts not connected to the God part.

OBTAINING WARRANTY SERVICE: Simply refer back to the Manufacturer's Guide (the Bible) to obtain much-needed refreshers and upgrades on a regular basis. This will keep your love connection intact. When in doubt, seek counsel from a source trained by the Manufacturer.

WARRANTY EXCLUSIVE: Either You believe God's promises or You don't. The only way this warranty will expire is if You choose to stop believing. Because of the power of the GOD part, know that long after you've run out of your capacity to love, His love endures forever. Should You decide to renew your agreement, simply realign yourself with this part to experience the ultimate love connection, thus empowering You to love at your greatest capacity. This warranty remains active and is available to consumers ad infinitum.

LIMITATION OR LIABILITY: The GOD part knows no limits. When You are plugged in to this part, all things are possible, no matter how much wear and tear the love unit has been subjected to. His work is guaranteed if His instructions are adhered to by two willing parts. If one part is unwilling, the process of making love work will prove difficult.

DISCLAIMER: If parts are not connected to the GOD part and do not follow the Manufacturer's Manual, anything can happen. Love's failure to work is then on You.

REGISTRATION

Name
Address
City _____ State _____ Zip_____

Date:
Signature:

 I agree to adhere to the instructions provided in the Manufacturer's Manual in order to ensure maximum performance of the love unit. Should I fail to follow the directions, I will accept all responsibility, holding no others liable for failure to operate.

'Tis a puzzlement
        A wonderment
An unspeakable glory
        The phenomenon of two
                Becoming one
Reflecting the three
        Father, Son, and Holy Ghost
Which are actually One
        Walking in complete agreement
                After their own counsel
That even though one was made in their image
                It is not good for man to be alone
        So fashioning another out of the one
                They joined them back together
Inserting themselves as One between the two
        Creating a three-fold cord
                That could not easily be broken . . .
'Tis profound
    That two could covenant to walk as one
                Having a good reward for their labor
                Loving when it hurts
Forgiving even when it is excruciating
        Pressing past each other's imperfections
                To pull one another up
                        To a higher revelation
'Tis unfathomable
        That two could love one another enough
To die over and over again
                        Year after year
                Month after month
                    Week after week
                        Day after day

Hour after hour
Minute after minute
Second after second
To everything that strives to
keep them separate . . .
'Tis extraordinary . . .
Remarkable
Intricately complex . . .
That man and woman
Can translate
What only angels see . . .
The deep mystery of
oneness . . .
'Tis awesome . . .
'Tis a miracle . . .
No . . . 'tis a tribute
To the grace of God
To be given a glimpse
Of what is to come . . .
To disclose the longing of the
Bridegroom . . .
That heaven would desire
To kiss the earth
And close the breadth between
Eternally joined forever and
ever
Amen . . .
Yes 'tis a tribute
To the manifold
Wonders of God
That He would create a
mystery
Within a mystery
This thing called marriage . . .

About the Author

Michelle McKinney Hammond is a bestselling author, speaker, relationship expert and empowerment coach, singer/songwriter, and television cohost. She is known for blending refreshing femininity with hard-hitting reality checks. She has written twenty-six books, including *The DIVA Principle* and the bestselling titles *Sassy, Single & Satisfied*, *Secrets of an Irresistible Woman*, and *101 Ways to Get and Keep His Attention*. You can find her Web site at www.michellehammond.com.